WITHDRAWN

a Wee Guide to

Rob Roy
MacGregor

MacGREGOR DESPITE THEM

a Wee Guide to

Rob Roy
MacGregor

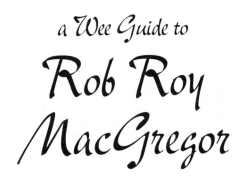

Charles Sinclair

GOBLINSHEAD

Musselburgh

a Wee Guide to Rob Roy MacGregor
© Martin Coventry 2000
Published by GOBLINSHEAD
130B Inveresk Road
Musselburgh EH21 7AY
Scotland
tel 0131 665 2894; *fax* 0131 653 6566; *email*
goblinshead@sol.co.uk

British Library Cataloguing in Publication Data
A catalogue record for this book is available from the British
Library.
ISBN 1 899874 32 1

Typeset by GOBLINSHEAD using Desktop Publishing

Wee Guides
William Wallace • The Picts • Scottish History
**Whisky • The Jacobites • Robert Burns • Prehistoric Scot-
land**
Mary, Queen of Scots • Robert the Bruce
Haunted Castles of Scotland • Macbeth and Early Scotland
Old Churches and Abbeys of Scotland
Castles and Mansions of Scotland
Due summer 2000
Rob Roy MacGregor
Scottish Ghosts and Bogles
Also published
Castles of Glasgow and the Clyde (£9.95)
Haunted Places of Scotland (£7.50)
The Hebrides (£5.95)
William Wallace – Champion of Scotland (£6.95)
Due summer 2000
The Castles of Scotland 3E (£15.95)
Myth and Magic (£7.50)

a Wee Guide to
Rob Roy MacGregor

Contents

List of Illustrations

Acknowledgements

Many thanks to everyone who helped in the production of this wee book including Martin and Joyce at Goblinshead for their hard work with the text and illustrations. Particular thanks to Sarah Seton at Argyll, the Isles, Loch Lomond, Stirling and the Trossachs Tourist Board for her help locating photos of Rob Roy MacGregor country. Isla Robertson at the NTS Picture Library and Helen Nicoll at the National Galleries were both extremely helpful. Thanks also to Hamish at Altered Images, Edinburgh for help with photo reproduction.

The following illustrations are reproduced by kind permission:
The National Portrait Gallery: Rob Roy MacGregor (R Cooper) frontispiece, p. 27, p. 76; Archibald Campbell, 1st Duke of Argyll (Peter Vanderbank) p. 30; James Graham, 1st Duke of Montrose (unknown) p. 47; James, Duke of York (P Lely) p. 22; John Erskine, Earl of Mar (Sir G Kneller) p. 52; John Graham, Viscount Dundee (unknown) p. 29; Battle of Glenshiel (Tillemans) front cover (detail), p. 65.
The National Trust of Scotland, Edinburgh: Killiecrankie p. 32; Glencoe p.98 and Culloden Memorial p. 72, p. 90.
Argyll, the Isles, Loch Lomond, Stirling and the Trossachs Tourist Board: Balfron p. 74; Balquhidder, general view p. 9; Finlarig Castle p. 97; Glen Dochart p. 51; Glen Fruin p. 14; Kilchurn Castle p. 11; Kippen p. 37; Loch Awe p. 7; Loch Katrine from Bed A'an p. 58; Loch Lomond from Dumpling p. 54; Old Kirk Balquhidder x 2 p. 61, p. 86; Rob Roy's statue, Stirling p. 67, p. 110; Rob Roy's grave, Balquhidder Old Kirk p. 69; Trossachs, general view p. 18.
Graham Coe: Balgonie Castle p. 85.
Drawings from MacGibbon and Ross: Castellated and Domestic Architecture of Scotland (1887-92).
Maps and design by Martin Coventry.

How to Use the Book

The book is divided into two sections:

• The text (pages 1-76) describes the background and principal events and people associated with Rob Roy MacGregor. Two maps (pages 4 and 26) locate the most important places mentioned in the text. A calendar of events summarises the period chronologically (pages 2-3).

• Places of interest, many of which can be visited, associated with Rob Roy MacGregor (pages 77-114) lists over 50 sites. There is a map (page 78) which illustrates their location, and a complete list (page 79). Information includes access, opening, facilities and a brief description. Admission charges are as follows: £ = £3.50 or under; ££ = £3.50-£5.00; £££ = more than £5.00.

An index (pages 115-118) lists all the main people, places and events.

Warning

While the information in this book was believed to be correct at time of going to press – and was checked, where possible, with the visitor attractions – opening times and facilities, or other information, may differ from that included. All information should be checked with the visitor attractions before embarking on any journey. Inclusion in the text is no indication whatsoever that a site is open to the public or that it should be visited. Some sites are in difficult and inaccessible locations, while ruinous buildings can be in a dangerous condition. Care should be taken when visiting any site. Inclusion or exclusion of any site should not be considered as a comment or judgement on that site. Locations on the maps are approximate.

Preface

Scotland in the late 17th and early 18th centuries was a place of turmoil, warfare and religious conflict. Added to this was widespread poverty and the increasing division between the Highlands and Lowlands, between the clans and the forces of 'law and order' – and between the MacGregors and the all-powerful Campbells.

Rob Roy was born into these times. The Stewart monarchs had a series of turbulent reigns, ending with James VII 'abdicating' and William of Orange replacing him as king. Many in Scotland tried to reinstate the Stewarts, and there were a series of Jacobite Risings, ending in the disaster of Culloden and the destruction of the Highland way of life.

Rob Roy was the third son of a chief of the MacGregors. Although he was involved with the Jacobites and fought at Killiecrankie, he was also a successful cattle dealer, drover and reiver. He held land on the east side of Loch Lomond and his prospects looked bright.

Bright, that is, until one of his men absconded with £1000 of borrowed money. Rob was declared bankrupt and his house was burnt and his wife cruelly used. He had no choice but to become an outlaw and rebel, and soon was a thorn in the side of the local magnates and landowners as well as the government.

This wee book covers his life and times, and attempts to put his deeds into a historical context. Rob remains one of the most compelling figures during the Jacobite Risings, both reiver and businessman, outlaw, rebel and outstanding leader.

It is also nice to write about a famous Scot who lived to a ripe old age.

CS, Musselburgh, April 2000.

a *Wee Guide to* Rob Roy MacGregor

MacGREGOR DESPITE THEM

Calendar of Events

1560   Gregor Roy is chief of the MacGregors.

1563   Colin Campbell of Glenorchy seizes family property; Gregor outlawed.

1566   Mary Queen of Scots grants the MacGregors peace.

1570   Gregor executed at Balloch (Taymouth).

1602/3   Slaughter of Lennox: MacGregors attack Colquhouns at Glen Fruin, Alasdair MacGregor outlawed and captured at Ardkinglas; Union of Crowns.

1604   Alasdair MacGregor hanged at Mercat Cross, Edinburgh; letters of Fire and Sword issued: clan name proscribed and outlawed.

1625   James VI dies and Charles I succeeds.

1642-6   Civil War; MacGregors fight for king; Charles I defeated; Cromwell governs England.

1649-50   Charles I executed; Charles II declared king by Scots; Scots defeated by Cromwell at Dunbar.

1660   Restoration of Charles II; repeals proscription of MacGregors

1671   Rob Roy MacGregor born.

1679   Unrest in Scotland; Battle of Drumclog; MacGregors fight for king at Battle of Bothwell Brig; Covenanters defeated.

1685   Charles II dies; succession of James VII.

1688   Birth of James Francis Edward 'the Old Pretender'; Revolution against James VII and II; James flees to France.

1689   William of Orange and Mary proclaimed joint monarchs; James VII's supporters led by Claverhouse; MacGregors led by Donald Glas (Rob Roy's father) join; Battle of Killiecrankie; Jacobites victorious but Claverhouse killed; Jacobites disband after defeat at Dunkeld; Donald Glas captured and imprisoned in Edinburgh. William reimposes proscription of MacGregors.

1690   Jacobites defeated at Cromdale; and at Battle of Boyne in Ireland.

1690-   Rob Roy and elder brother Iain command Lennox Watch.

1691   Margaret Campbell, Rob Roy's mother, dies; Donald Glas signs Oath of Allegiance to William in return for his freedom; 'Hership of Kippen' - raid on Kippen led by Rob Roy.

1692   Massacre of Glencoe.

1693   Rob Roy and Helen Mary MacGregor of Comer marry; reintroduction of proscription against MacGregors.

1695-1700   Company of Scotland formed; disaster of Darien Scheme. Rob Roy and Mary's first son born; Rob arrested in Glasgow but escapes. Iain MacGregor dies.

1701   Death of James VII and II; Act of Settlement: Crown to go to Hanoverian George; Rob Roy acquires land at Craigrostan.

1702   William of Orange dies, succeeded by Anne. Donald Glas, Rob Roy's father, dies. Rob continues to work as cattle drover and trader.

1707   Union of Scottish and English parliaments.

1708   Aborted campaign for James VIII to return to Scotland; Rob acquires more property at Rowardennan.

1712   Rob's drover, Duncan MacDonald, absconds with money and letters of credit from Montrose; Montrose declares Rob thief and bankrupt; summoned to appear in Edinburgh; declared outlaw.

1713   Montrose's men evict Rob's family from Craigrostan; Rob leases land at Auchinchisallen.

1714   Queen Anne dies; succession of George I.

1715-16   Standard raised for James VIII and III at Braemar by Earl of Mar; Rob Roy and MacGregors join Jacobite side; Battle of Sheriffmuir; James VIII lands at Peterhead; Rob Roy takes Falkland Palace and raids Fife; Jacobites disband; James VIII returns to France; Rob Roy accused of treason; Rob Roy hands over old guns and weapons to Argyll; settles at Glen Shira.

1717   Rob Roy raids Montrose's lands; Letter of Fire and Sword issued and Rob captured at Balquhidder; escapes on way to Stirling; taken prisoner at Dunkeld but escapes from Logierait.

1718   Property at Inversnaid seized by Commissioners for Confiscated Estates; converted to barracks.

1719   Rob involved in Jacobite campaign; Eilean Donan Castle used as base; Battle of Glen Shiel; Jacobites defeated; Rob returns to Glen Shira.

1720   Rob moves family to Inverlochlarig at Balquhidder; commands the Lennox Watch; birth of Bonnie Prince Charlie: Charles Edward 'the Young Pretender'.

1723   Daniel Defoe publishes *Highland Rogue*, fictionalised account of Rob Roy's exploits.

1725   Rob sends letter of submission to George I.

1730   Rob converts to catholicism.

1734   Death of Rob Roy MacGregor.

1745   Bonnie Prince Charlie arrives in Scotland; James Mor MacGregor, Rob's eldest son, fights at Prestonpans; Colonel Gardiner slain by a MacGregor.

1746   Jacobite victory at Battle of Falkirk; James MacGregor fights at defeat of Culloden; severe retribution against Highlanders.

1750   Robin Oig MacGregor, with his brothers, kidnap Jean Kay and force her to marry him.

1752   MacGregor brothers tried for abduction and forcible marriage: Robin Oig executed, James Mor escapes, and Duncan found not guilty.

1754   James Mor dies in Paris.

1774   End of proscription of the MacGregors; John Murray of Lanrick chosen as clan chief.

1786   Ranald MacGregor, last surviving son of Rob Roy, dies.

Map 1: Scotland 1633-1707
Also see Map 2 (page 26)

ORKNEY

Kirkwall

Thurso

Wick

LEWIS

Stornoway

Ullapool

HARRIS

Dornoch

NORTH
UIST

Fraserburgh

Elgin

Peterhead

SOUTH
UIST

SKYE

Inverness

Castle Grant
✕ Cromdale
(1690)

Aberdeen

BARRA

Glen Roy

Dunnottar
Mearns

Fort William
(Inverlochy)

Blair Cas.

✕ Killiecrankie
(1689)

Montrose

Glencoe

Dunkeld

Angus

MULL

Glenstrae *Breadalbane*

Dundee

Iona

Oban

Perth

Fife

St Andrews

Inveraray

Glengyle
The Trossachs

JURA

Glen Fruin (1603) ✕

Menteith

Stirling

Kirkcaldy

Dunbar

Dumbarton

Lennox

Edinburgh

(1650)

ISLAY

Glasgow

✕ Rullion Green

BUTE

Drumclog
(1679) ✕

Bothwell
Brig (1679)

Berwick

Melrose

ARRAN

Ayr

Philiphaugh
(1645)

ENGLAND

Dumfries

Stranraer

1-Royal is My Race

The history of the MacGregors.

Rob Roy MacGregor is one of the most well-known of Scottish figures. Unlike Mary Queen of Scots, Robert the Bruce, Bonnie Prince Charlie – or even William Wallace – he was not of noble blood. It is true that he held lands, but his fame – or notoriety – was earned by his own resourcefulness, charisma and exploits. His life was made all the more difficult by the poverty, strife and confusion of the time.

Scotland had gone through a period of religious turmoil since the start of the Reformation in 1560. Many in Scotland wanted a presbyterian church, and this led to conflict with James VI and later Stewart monarchs who preferred an episcopalian system. This system allowed them to remain as head of the church and appoint bishops as they wished.

Also, while the Reformation led to lands and money being taken from the church and given to lairds and nobles, it was not necessarily distributed among the rest of the population. Indeed there was much hardship and increasing poverty in both the Highlands and the Lowlands, partly due to warfare and strife, partly to the general economic conditions of the time. The MacGregors had to deal with the powerful Campbells, the Earls and Dukes of Argyll and of Breadalbane, and gradually lost lands. There were other clans who also fared badly at the hands of the Campbells: the MacNaughtons, MacEwens, MacDougalls, MacNabs, MacLeans and even the MacDonalds. Eventually the Campbells controlled virtually all of Argyll and elsewhere and made it their fiefdom. In order to survive, the MacGregors turned increasingly to blackmail and reiving, in turn giving the Campbells further excuse to harry, outlaw and hunt the 'Children of the Mist', all but extinguishing the clan.

The MacGregors are one of the oldest clans of Scotland, the *Gregorach* or Children of the Mist. For hundreds of years they held lands in Argyll and Perthshire: the three glens of Glenorchy, Glenstrae and Glenlochy. Little is known for certain about their early history, although there are legends about their origins.

One is that the clan is descended from Grigor, one of the sons of Alpin, who was King of Scots around 787. Alpin was slain by the Picts, but was father of Kenneth MacAlpin, who finally united the Scots and Picts under one king – although the royal houses of the two kingdoms had been intermarrying for years. The clan slogan is *'S Rioghal mo dhream* or 'Royal is my race' and this is said to come from this connection. Many claim there is little in fact to support this story. Another tale behind their origin is that they are descended from Griogair, son of Dungal, reputedly a lesser king or ruler around 880. Another that they were directly related to the hereditary Bishops of Glendochart who were of royal lineage.

There are also a number of stories concerning later MacGregors, yet still early in Scottish history. Some time after 1066, Sir John MacGregor of Glenorchy married a beautiful English lady. She had came to Scotland with Queen Margaret, fleeing from England after the invasion by William the Conqueror. Margaret was the sister of the heir to the English throne, and she married Malcolm III, more usually known as Malcolm Canmore.

MacGregor's son was known as 'Malcolm of the Castles', and may have built the original castle at Kilchurn as well as a moated stronghold at Stronmilchan, at the mouth of Glenstrae, and other strongholds. He reputedly saved Malcolm Canmore, or one of his sons or grandsons, from a wild boar by fighting it off with a tree until he could kill it. The arms of the chief traditionally bear an oak tree rather than the Scots Pine badge of the clan.

John MacGregor of Glenorchy was captured following the disastrous Battle of Dunbar in 1296, when the Scottish army was defeated by the English and Edward I. He was imprisoned in France where he died.

John had no sons, and his daughter and heiress married John, son of Neil Campbell of Loch Awe. The barony remained with the MacGregors, and Malcolm MacGregor, acting as chief, fought for Robert the Bruce at the Battle of Bannockburn in 1314. Malcolm accompanied Edward Bruce to Ireland – Edward, Robert's brother, was briefly High King of Ireland. Malcolm was badly wounded at Dundalk and then known as 'the lame'.

Rather setting the cat among the pigeons, Bruce granted the barony of Loch Awe, which included much of the MacGregor lands, to Neil Campbell who was a close friend and captain of the king. This must have seemed a rather odd way to reward the MacGregor's loyalty. There was already a stronghold, Kilchurn Castle at the Pass of Brander near Glenstrae, which helped control the western

Loch Awe and the Pass of Brander.

Highlands. It was probably built by the MacGregors, but seized by the Campbells. Over many centuries, both openly and by stealth, the Campbells attacked the MacGregors, and forced them to withdraw, weakening them, and taking MacGregor lands for their own.

The first recorded (and therefore historical) chief of the MacGregors was Gregor 'of the golden bridles', who died before 1390. He was succeeded by his son, Iain Camm One-Eye. John Dubh (the 'Black') died in 1415, and his sons inherited parts of MacGregor estates. From them were descended the MacGregors of Roro, of Glengyle, and of Brackly.

Around 1450 Duncan, Lord Campbell, acquired the superiority over the MacGregor land. He passed Glenorchy to his son Colin, so founding the Campbells of Breadalbane, who later rose to be Earls and major land owners. Glenstrae, he kept, with the MacGregors as vassals to the Campbells.

Iain MacGregor of Glenstrae, also called 'the Black', died in 1519. Unfortunately for his clan, he had no direct male heirs. John MacGregor of Brackly, who had a good claim, was not recognised as chief. The Campbells decided to support Eian MacGregor, who had married a daughter of Sir Colin Campbell of Glenorchy.

This could well have been a deliberate policy of the often devious Campbells. Whether or not, it fell to their advantage. The MacGregors turned on each other, and the confusion weakened them and strengthened their superiors.

The MacGregors' increasing lack of land and property led to poverty and hardship. In order to survive they had to thieve and lift cattle from their own former lands, further pushing them outside the law. This in turn meant that the Campbells could denounce them as thieves and brigands, and further weaken their position. Despite all this, the clan remained loyal to the Crown. In 1547 Alasdair, Eian's son,

Balquhidder.

fought at the Battle of Pinkie, another Scottish defeat at the hands of the English, although he died shortly afterwards.

The MacGregors were quite capable of a bit of murder themselves. It is recorded that in 1558 the chief of the MacLarens and many of his folk were slaughtered in 'the midnight hour' by the MacGregors. The MacLarens held much lands around Balquhidder and Strathearn.

The Reformation came to Scotland around the middle of the 16th century. The Roman catholic church was denounced as corrupt, both morally and spiritually, and the protestant ideas of Luther and Calvin found increasing support, at least in Lowland areas. The Reformers eventually declared Scotland a protestant country in 1560. But although abbeys and priories were dissolved and their property taken over by the Crown, the structure and organisation of the church was not settled. By Rob Roy's time the MacGregors were protestants.

Gregor Roy, second son of Alasdair, should have succeeded

as chief of the MacGregors following the death of his older brother. Indeed, he came of age in 1560, but Sir Colin Campbell of Glenorchy, refused to recognise his claim. Three years later Campbell even arranged to receive a government grant of all the MacGregors' remaining property. Gregor Roy could do nothing at this time, and had no alternative but to become an outlaw. He survived by stealing cattle and hiding in the glens, aided by his own clansmen, some of whom still had land under the Campbells. Their reiving was not confined to Campbell lands, however, and many of their neighbours were also made to suffer. The fortunes of the clan were sinking, and there was little they could do to turn the tide.

Because he had been outlawed and had nothing to lose, Gregor Roy decided to offer his services to the Crown. In 1565 the sons of the Dean of Lismore had been murdered. Gregor Roy was given a warrant from Mary Queen of Scots to find and kill the assassins. In return the following year Mary accepted the clan into her peace, and even arranged that the laird of Weem would rent them lands around Loch Rannoch.

This could not have pleased the Campbells, but unfortunately for the MacGregors, Mary had her own troubles. Her marriage to Darnley ended in his murder, and her marriage to Bothwell was a disaster. She was imprisoned and forced to abdicate in 1567, and although she escaped she was defeated at the Battle of Langside and thereafter fled to England. Conflict between Mary's party (the Queen's party – although she was imprisoned in England by Elizabeth from 1568) and the King's Party simmered away until 1573, with the defeat of the last of Mary's supporters. Mary was eventually beheaded by the English in 1587.

Meanwhile, the Campbells seized their opportunity, but the MacGregors reacted in the only way left to them: violently. They were a hard-bitten lot and years of persecution had produced many fine fighting men from the clan – they were not going to disappear without a fight.

Forces were mustering against them, and in 1569 a bond was signed by the Earls of Atholl, Glenorchy, and others, to crush the MacGregors. Gregor Roy was harried and pursued, and with his wife Marion, daughter of Campbell of Glenlyon, was forced to go into hiding. They sought refuge in a cave above Loch Tay. But they were discovered, and Gregor Roy was seized by Glenorchy's men. No mercy was shown, and Gregor Roy was executed at Balloch Castle (which is now known as Taymouth) on 7 April 1570.

Alasdair Roy, who had been raised in Glenstrae, was his heir but could do little to improve matters, although he was a strong and skilful character. In 1590 he was implicated in the murder of John Drummond, the king's forester. Drummond reputedly hanged some MacGregors for poaching, and in revenge was slain by others of the clan. Although Alasdair probably had no hand in the killing, as chief he took responsibility. Things, however, seemed to be improving when James VI pardoned him in 1596.

James had been crowned king in 1567, although he was

Kilchurn Castle at the mouth of Glenstrae.

only an infant, and Scotland was ruled by a succession of regents. Although his mother Mary had been a catholic, James was brought up as a protestant. In 1585 the 20 year-old James took control of the kingdom. Not that Scotland was by any means a peaceful and settled place: James had been kidnapped by his own protestant nobles in 1582, there was a catholic rising in Scotland, led by the Earl of Huntly, in 1594, and an apparent plot to kidnap or kill James at Gowrie House in Perth in 1600.

It became increasingly clear that James was going to ascend to the throne of England as well as Scotland. The Virgin Queen, Elizabeth of England, was unwed and had produced no children. This meant that James was next in line to the English crown (his great grandfather James IV had married Margaret Tudor, sister to Henry VIII of England).

The bad luck of the clan, however, continued, exacerbated by the ill will of the Campbells and the sometimes hot-headed actions of the MacGregors themselves.

A difficult situation arose in 1602 when two MacGregors were refused hospitality. They arrived at Luss, on the banks of Loch Lomond, and looked for lodging and food. But Sir Alexander Colquhoun, the laird, refused and turned them away from his doors.

This may have had something to do with the events at

The ruins of Bannachra Castle.

Bannachra some years before in 1592. The MacGregors were besieging the castle. Sir Humphrey Colquhoun was sheltering here and in no great danger from his enemies. On his way to bed, however, he was illuminated in one of the windows by a treacherous servant. One of the Mac-Gregors shot him with an arrow and Sir Humphrey was killed. The castle was then taken and torched.

Nevertheless, Sir Alexander Colquhoun's actions were still a breach of Highland hospitality. The MacGregors stole a sheep which they killed and ate and, although the MacGregors offered to pay for the beast, Colquhoun had them executed on the spot.

When the news got back to Alasdair, he was greatly angered and it was certain that the clan could not let the matter rest. So in revenge, in that December, a raiding party of MacGregors attacked Rossdhu Castle. They killed two men and lifted three hundred cows and a large number of sheep, goats and horses.

Colquhoun took the matter to James VI. A number of Colquhoun women showed the king their reputedly murdered husbands' bloody sarks (shirts) as evidence of Mac-Gregor brutality. This was orchestrated, exaggerated (there were scores of 'widows' but apparently only two deaths), and may have been at the instigation of the Campbells.

Then early in 1603 the MacGregors raided again, reportedly slaying many and burning Luss. Inevitably it came to battle. Colquhoun with about 800 of his own clan and the Buchanans headed towards Loch Long and the withdrawing MacGregors. Alasdair probably had half the number of MacGregors, Camerons and MacDonalds, but the resulting battle in Glen Fruin on 17 February was a rout. The MacGregors and their allies slew more than 140, perhaps as many as 200, of Colquhoun's men.

James VI had granted Colquhoun Letters of Fire and Sword against the MacGregors, and after the Battle of Glen Friun, the matter was reported to the Privy Council. In April 1603 James proclaimed the name of MacGregor 'altogidder abolisheed', meaning that those who bore the name must renounce it or suffer death.

Alasdair was captured at Ardkinglas but managed to escape as he was being taken from Loch Fyne to Inveraray. However, perhaps rather surprisingly and foolishly as it turned out, he surrendered himself to the Campbell Earl of Argyll.

Glen Fruin – site of the battle.

Alasdair had sought Argyll's advice regarding the Colquhoun problem. If Alasdair's dying statement is to be believed, Argyll had actually encouraged him to raid Colquhoun lands and was at least partly responsible for the slaughter at Glen Fruin. Alasdair may have believed that Argyll would support him, or at least ensure that he could escape to England. Instead Argyll persuaded Alasdair to go to Edinburgh and plead his case for himself and for his clan. When he got to the capital, however, Alasdair and his men were thrown into prison. Alasdair was hanged at Edinburgh's Mercat Cross in early 1604 accompanied by five of his clan chiefs, while another six were hanged in February and March.

That was not where the punishment stopped. Another declaration of Fire and Sword was issued against the MacGregors. Anyone and everyone could – and indeed were duty bound to – kill, harry, burn and dispossess any MacGregors they might find. This might not have proved that easy, however, as it seems unlikely the MacGregors would not have retaliated as they were renowned fighters.

The very name of MacGregor was proscribed and effectively abolished. This meant it was impossible for anyone of that name to hold land or sign legal documents. Consequently the MacGregors then took on other names such as Graham, Greig, Gregory, Grier, Grierson, Carse, Cass, Fletcher, Drummond, Grant and even Campbell. This is why there are no so many different family names connected with the MacGregor clan.

The MacGregors were looking for revenge for the hanging of their chief and ravaged across the Campbell lands of Glenorchy and Breadalbane, and raided Fortingall and Menteith. They torched Achallader Castle. The MacGregors believed that their downfall was planned by the Campbells, and in this they were probably right.

Not all clans wanted to be on poor terms with the MacGregors. Much in Highland history was based on 'your enemy's enemy is my friend' and the Campbells were becoming dominant and increasingly unpopular. It was probably also preferable to have the MacGregors as friends than to have them raiding your lands, so approaches were made to the clan. In 1624 about 300 members MacGregors were taken north from Menteith by the Earl of Moray. Moray had problems with the Macintoshes and Clan Chattan.

As stated before, the MacGregors were renowned for their fighting prowess, and many of the clan settled in Aberdeenshire, Moray and elsewhere – some even ended up in Applecross in Wester Ross.

2-The Scotland of Rob Roy MacGregor

Political and religious background.

When Elizabeth of England died James VI of Scots also became king James I of England. He left for London in 1603, only returning to Scotland once. This united the crowns of Scotland and England, although it was to do little to unite the countries otherwise.

The two kingdoms maintained separate parliaments and church organisation. The religious settlement was not straightforward. From 1592 there had been some attempt to establish a presbyterian form of church government in Scotland. This system did not have bishops and the church was organised by elected representative members: both lay and clerical. This system also rejected the monarch as head of the church, declaring that God had ultimate supremacy, even over a monarch. In reaction to this James imposed an episcopal church, which caused resentment. This allowed him to select bishops and keep control over ecclesiastical matters. James also managed to stop reiving in the Scottish borders. He dealt harshly with border families and many of them later settled in the north of Ireland.

The 7th Earl of Argyll, as Justice-General, was left in charge. Argyll was James's representative, but also had his own agenda: to increase the property and influence of the Campbells. His attention was turned on the MacDonalds, and he raided Islay burning and plundering: the island then passed into the hands of the Campbells.

He could also be more subtle when required. Argyll invited many clan chiefs to Iona, but then had them arrested. They were not freed until 1609 when they agreed to what later became known as the Bond and Statutes of Iona. The

Iona.

articles of this Covenant were proscriptive. Protestant churches were to be established, English was to be used instead of Gaelic, the distilling of whisky and importing of wine was banned, firearms were prohibited, and bards and story tellers were to be suppressed. This latter measure may seem odd, but Highland culture, oral in tradition, was spread by wandering bards and this was another way of reducing the influence of Gaelic traditions. Whether Argyll or James VI really thought they could impose these measures is questionable, and it would not be for another 150 years and the Battle of Culloden that the Highland way of life was extinguished.

When James died in 1625, his son Charles I inherited the two crowns. Charles did not rule well, and he became increasingly unpopular, both in Scotland and England. Part of this was because of his continued imposition of the episcopalian church and his determination to control such matters. There were protests, including a riot at St Giles Cathedral in Edinburgh. His behaviour, perceived arrogance and other measures led to much discontent, both among the nobility and general populace. This led to the writing and signing of what is known as the National Covenant. This document asserted the power of the people over the monarch in their right to choose how the church was organised.

Many of the MacGregors had no choice but to live on the edge or outside the law. In 1633 it had again become legal to kill Mac-Gregors and to hunt them with blood-h o u n d s. Charles I issued a Letter of Fire and Sword and declared that, although the MacGregors had been broken by James VI, in recent years they had com-

The Trossachs.

mitted raids in Menteith, Angus, Clackmannan, the Lennox, the Mearns, Perth and Stirling. Their activities centred around the Trossachs and Glengyle.

Shortly, Charles was to have more pressing problems as England and Scotland descended into conflict.

There had been simmering discontent for several years, but things came to a head when civil war broke out in 1642. Despite being treated badly by virtually all the Stewart monarchs, some 1000 MacGregors, led by Patrick MacGregor of Glenstrae, fought for Charles I during the

Civil War. This may have been based on some residual and misplaced loyalty. To a large part, however, it was because the Earl of Argyll was opposed to the king.

In Scotland the Marquis of Montrose led an effective rising for the king and won a string of victories of 1644-5. The MacGregors had joined the Marquis of Montrose in his campaign. Montrose, in turn, supported the clan's claim for the restoration of their titles and lands. Charles was defeated in England in 1645, and Montrose continued south, but with fewer and fewer men as many left for the harvest. So it was that his small army was surprised by a Covenanter force, led by David Leslie, at Philiphaugh in 1645. His army was routed, and many of his men and campfollowers were massacred after the battle, although Montrose himself escaped. Leslie then led a punitive campaign up the west coast of Scotland.

Charles's cause was failing. By 1646 Charles and the Royalist side had been defeated by the Parliamentarians led by Cromwell, who was supported by some Scots. The king was captured and turned over to the English and imprisoned. Then in 1649, without consulting the Scots, the English executed Charles I by beheading.

There was anger in Scotland, uniting the kingdom against Cromwell, so much so that Charles II was proclaimed king by the Scots. They rose against Cromwell, but the resistance, lacking the military leadership of Montrose and driven by clerics rather than soldiers, was badly managed. Although the Scottish army was led by the experienced general, David Leslie, Cromwell crushed the Scots at the Battle of Dunbar in 1650. Charles II was crowned King of Scots at Scone a year later (and, it should be pointed out, signed the National Covenant), but Cromwell was sweeping across Scotland. Dunnottar, the last northern stronghold, had fallen by 1652 and Scotland became part of the

Dunnottar Castle.

Cromwellian Commonwealth. Charles II fled to the continent.

There was another rising against Cromwell, led by the Earl of Glencairn, some two years later. The MacGregors took part, supplying some 200 men – but the rebellion came to nothing.

In 1660, after Cromwell's death and the collapse of the Commonwealth, Charles II was invited to return to Britain and become King of England, Wales and Scotland. Charles II and his brother James, Duke of York, returned to England, and the new king appointed John Maitland, Duke of Lauderdale, as Secretary of State for Scotland: Charles never visited Scotland after 1660, and Lauderdale virtually ruled the country for the next 20 years. However, his administration was not without problems and conflict.

Episcopacy was again introduced to Scotland, although Charles II had signed the National Covenant in 1651 – he claimed he was forced to do so against his will. Conventicles, prayer and preaching gatherings of groups of Covenanters, were outlawed. Religious strife and intolerance continued.

This led to the Pentland Rising by the Covenanters in 1666, which was extinguished at the Battle of Rullion Green. An amnesty was announced in 1667 for those who would swear not to bear arms against the king.

Nevertheless unrest continued and, despite being outlawed, conventicles spread. The 'Highland Host' were quartered on Covenanters in the south-west in an attempt to force them into line. This was hugely unpopular, and hardly improved things: Archbishop John Sharp, head of the Episcopalian church, was violently murdered by Covenanters. He was dragged from his carriage and was shot, slashed, trampled and had his skull crushed.

In Scotland the situation continued to worsen, culminating in a battle on 1 June 1679 at Drumclog, near Strathaven. John Graham of Claverhouse – who was later to take a major part in the first of the Jacobite Risings – and a force of government soldiers were defeated by a heavily-armed party of Covenanters. The Covenanters were heartened by the victory and their support grew. They quickly raised an army, although their victory was short lived and they were soon divided by dissent. At the Battle of Bothwell Brig, at which the MacGregors fought, on 22 June 1679, they were routed by government troops led by James Duke of Monmouth and Claverhouse.

Lauderdale was replaced as Secretary of State by James Duke of Monmouth, illegitimate son of Charles II, then by James Duke of York, who was later James VII. During the latter's period of office persecution of Covenanters increased, many were summarily executed, and this became known as the Killing Times.

Charles II died in 1685. He had achieved two objectives: he had survived as monarch of both England and Scotland; and strengthened the position of the Crown. He had also secured the succession of his brother, despite the fact that James was openly a Roman Catholic. It was in keeping

James VII when Duke of York (P. Lely).

with the rest of the Stewarts that James then managed to make a complete mess of things

James was proclaimed King of Scots on 10 February 1685 at the age of 51; but, although he promised 'to defend and support' the Episcopalian Church of England, he refused to take the Scottish Coronation Oath to defend the protestant religion. When Parliament met in April a new Act once more declared supporting the Covenant to be treason, and attendance at conventicles punishable by death.

The failure of Monmouth's rising – which was supported in Scotland by Archibald Campbell, 9th Earl of Argyll, who was no friend of the MacGregors – strengthened James's position. Argyll was captured and beheaded after the failure of the rebellion, and rival clans took the opportunity to plunder his lands. Monmouth's campaign in the south of England was no more successful, and he was beheaded on Tower Hill in London.

But the birth of a son James Francis Edward – 'the Old Pretender' – on 10 June was too much for the English, and Covenanters and others in Scotland. It focused attention on James and his religion. Many now believed that James's catholic policies would continue after his death: that a new Roman Catholic dynasty would be founded. The answer was simple.

William of Orange, James's nephew and a staunch protestant, landed at Torbay on 5 November, and he was supported by many disaffected Scots. James was surprised by this turn of events, panicked and eventually fled to France on 23 December. It was claimed that by fleeing he had abdicated and had left the throne vacant. William accepted the English throne on 13 February 1689. That was it. The throne for which the Jacobites then so doggedly fought had been lost so easily.

William of Orange had married Mary – his own cousin and daughter of James VII – in 1677 (when she was just 15: the couple do not appear to have been close and they had no children). William, however, had left Mary behind when he arrived in England, demanding that he be made joint sovereign with her or he would return to Holland. He, in turn, agreed that questions of Church and State should be settled by a free parliament, and so the English proclaimed him king.

Scottish Episcopalians had no wish to be ruled by William, a Dutch protestant, and many others, both in Scotland and England, remained loyal to James; but the Scots were surprised and divided by James's flight. William agreed to a convention of the Scottish Estates, although he did not attend. The meeting was held on 14 March 1689. Claverhouse, now Viscount Dundee and loyal to

James, returned from England to attend the Convention.

The delegates were split, and the two claimants presented letters. William's letter was relatively moderate and conciliatory; James's, on the other hand, was essentially a threat of vengeance on anyone who did not support their rightful monarch. Not surprisingly James's letter upset many waverers, even episcopalians, into thinking he might be going to restore the authority of the Pope. The Convention was now decided: divided into a small number of committed Jacobites, led by Claverhouse, and a much larger group who supported William. They may have been helped in their decision by the presence of an armed force, led by MacKay of Scourie, which supported William.

Claverhouse was outlawed by the Convention in Edinburgh on 30 March. He travelled north into the Highlands where there was a large number of Jacobite supporters, or at least those who saw their fortunes served by a war.

On 4 April 1689 the Estates issued a 'Declaration'. This was a claim of right and an offer of the throne to William of Orange and Mary. It stated that James had 'for-faulted' or forfeited his right as king, and the throne was therefore vacant. It also laid down some conditions: that only a protestant could be monarch, there was to be no taxation without the consent of parliament, and the monarch could not be above the laws of the country. A new Coronation Oath was also drawn up, and as a result William and Mary were offered the throne provided they upheld the laws, religion and liberties of the Scottish people. William agreed to the Declaration, and took the Oath on 11 May 1689, confirming both himself and Mary as joint monarchs.

Scotland may have had a new protestant monarch but the final outcome was by no means settled. The Jacobites continued to pursue their aim of reestablishing the Stewart monarchy and many families and clans, including the

MacGregors, supported their cause.

The MacGregors had declared their support for James when they had taken the Oath of Allegiance and, along with other clans, attempted to prevent Campbell of Argyll administering the coronation oath for William of Orange. This just goes to show the contradictory allegiances of the day: the protestant MacGregors would support a catholic king over the protestant William of Orange.

As a result, the proscription of the MacGregors, of course, was reimposed. The clan was, once again, on the wrong side of the law. It was with this background that the young Rob Roy emerged onto the Scottish scene.

Map 2: Rob Roy's Scotland 1671-1746
Also see Map 1 (page 4)

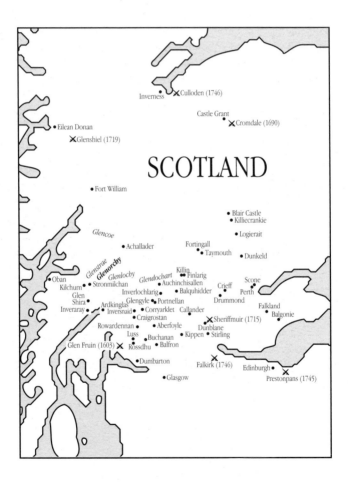

3-*Early Years 1671-1701*

Rob Roy and the Jacobites.

Rob Roy MacGregor was so named because of his red hair – 'roy' (or *ruadh*) is from the Gaelic for red. He was born in 1671 by the banks of Loch Katrine in the Trossachs area of Stirlingshire, part of the Scottish Highlands. Rob was the third son of Donald – Donald Glas – MacGregor of Glengyle and Margaret Campbell, his wife. He had two older brothers, Iain and Duncan. Donald Glas was descended from the Glenorchy branch of his family, and was a chief of the MacGregors.

Rob had lands at Inversnaid, on the east side of Loch Lomond, although it is not clear when he acquired them. He is said to have had extremely long arms, and was widely

Etching, believed to be of Rob Roy (unknown).

known for his expertise with the broadsword. He spoke Gaelic, although he was also literate in English, and was brought up in the clan system. This meant as well as being an expert swordsman, he was well trained as a drover and, of course, a cattle reiver. Rob was particularly skilled and successful at both: these two occupations were closely linked. Cattle reiving was widespread, in particular when beasts were on their way to market – after all, why go to the trouble and expense of fattening your own beasts when you get others to fatten theirs before lifting them.

Rob and the MacGregors would protect the cattle of other clans and families, and drive them through difficult areas to market. In return they received payment, either money, goods or 'meal', known as blackmail or black rent. Those who preferred to keep their money and drive their own cattle were in severe danger of having them stolen, often by the MacGregors. This was not due to any character defect in the clans – it was an economic necessity.

The Highlands were regarded increasingly as lawless compared to the 'sophisticated' and 'peaceful' Lowlands – an interesting analysis as the Lowlands had been riven by decades of bloody religious and civil wars.

The two areas were differentiated by more than perception, geography and economy – the differences were pronounced. Highland dress was different: clansmen wore a plaid (which was later developed into the kilt for Scottish regiments in the British army) rather than trousers. It was easier to walk through damp heather and grass in a short 'skirt' than in trousers which soaked up water. The language and culture of the Highlands were also different: Gaelic, bardic poetry and pipe music were integral to society, despite the efforts of the government and the Bond and Statutes of Iona. Clans were paternalistic – the chief had absolute say in matters of law and over his clansmen. Highland society had its customs and rules regarding loyalty, hospitality and warfare. Religion was a further difference. While Highlanders were mostly Roman catholic or episcopalian, Lowlanders were usually protestant and presbyterian.

Where the two were united was in poverty. The economy and agriculture of Scotland were both poor. In the Lowlands, towns were crowded and full of disease, but rural areas also suffered from war, illness – including several outbreaks of plague – and hunger.

William and Mary were confirmed as joint monarchs in 1689, and their position was reasonably secure. There was little unrest in England: perhaps the English remained unimpressed with the Scottish Stewart monarchs. In Scotland things were different. James VII still commanded strong support throughout many parts of Scotland, not just the Highlands, and of course from John Graham of Claverhouse, also known as 'Bonnie Dundee'. This was extended to his son, James Francis Edward Stewart 'the

John Graham of Claverhouse (unknown artist).

Archibald Campbell, 10th Earl and 1st Duke of Argyll (Peter Vanderbank).

Old Pretender'. These supporters were known as Jacobites, from the Latin for James.

This may seem strange given their history of persecution and strife, and given that Scotland was strongly protestant and James was a confirmed catholic. This loyalty was also, of course, in part due in part to an intense dislike and distrust of the English, and their often high-handed ways with their smaller and less-powerful neighbour. The Jacobite cause attracted a rag-tag bunch of supporters, both catholics and protestants. William of Orange was also extremely unpopular, which helped the Jacobites no end.

One reason for this was the support for William of Orange by the Campbell Earl of Argyll. Many other smaller or weaker clans – protestant, catholic or episcopalian – had suffered at the hands of the Campbells, and so supported the Jacobites. Which is a shame: the Stewart monarchs cared little for the Highlands or its clans other than as a source of good fighting men.

Following the acceptance of William and Mary as joint monarchs, Graham of Claverhouse, Viscount Dundee, went north to rally support for James. Donald Glas and his family supported James, as did many others of the MacGregor clan. Donald Glas had taken the Oath of Allegiance and was a man of honour. Claverhouse, as James's Lieutenant General, raised an army. This was mostly made up of clans: MacDonalds, Camerons, Stewarts and MacLeans – and MacGregors. Donald Glas and Rob Roy had joined Claverhouse as he marshalled his forces at Blair. Rob was just 18.

Blair Castle, the home of John Murray, Marquis of Atholl, was seized by Claverhouse. Atholl had been loyal to the Stewarts but now, although he did not support William and Mary, he would not join the Jacobites, perhaps feeling it would best serve his own interests to hedge his bets. His younger son, however, was more willing to commit himself and supported James. He made sure that Claverhouse captured the castle.

A government army, led by General Hugh MacKay of Scourie, marched north from Stirling to recover Blair, and then strengthen the garrison Inverlochy (renamed Fort William in honour of William of Orange). Two thousand Jacobites swept down from Glen Roy to gather near Blair, while MacKay reached nearby Dunkeld on 26 July.

The next day MacKay advanced through the narrow Pass of Killiecrankie towards Blair, but found the Jacobites positioned on the lower slopes of Creag Eallaich. The Jacobites overlooked MacKay's army and the two forces waited; Claverhouse biding his time before starting his attack. The government artillery fired on the Jacobites – although it is reported they only managed nine shots. There

Killiecrankie.

was no response from the Jacobites. Claverhouse waited for evening until the sun was low in the sky. Finally the Jacobites were ordered to charge. MacKay's men fired, but the charge was not checked. Much of the government army was then swept away and routed by the fierce clansmen. The Pass of Killiecrankie streamed with fleeing government troops, and many drowned in the River Garry.

General MacKay made a last desperate stand. Claverhouse led the attack, but was brought down by a musket-ball. His men were driven off and he is said to have been slain by a looter as he lay wounded. After the battle his body was taken to Blair Castle to be buried in the nearby churchyard of old St Bride's. Indeed, casualties were heavy on both sides: MacKay is thought to have lost 2000 men. Rob and his father fought at Killiecrankie and survived

MacKay, himself, managed to retreat, rallying a small number of his men and leading them southwards towards Weem. Although the Jacobites were victorious, the death of Claverhouse was a serious blow – indeed it was to prove disastrous.

The Jacobites were then led by an Irish professional soldier, Colonel Cannon. Their army, swollen by new recruits from the Murray, Robertson, Menzies and Stewart clans of Atholl, as well as the Farquharsons, Macphersons, Frasers and Gordons, moved on to attack Dunkeld. The town was defended by Cameronians, men who were implacably hostile to the Stewarts. Dunkeld was devastated in the following siege, and mostly burnt to the ground. Both sides lost many men. William Clelland, the young Colonel of the Cameronians, was killed, but Cannon was not as able a leader as Claverhouse and could not pierce the defences. The Cameronians were victorious, and the Jacobite forces retreated and disbanded, raiding the Campbell lands of Breadalbane as they withdrew. The rising had suffered a serious setback: despite winning the Battle of Killiecrankie, they were in danger of losing the war.

Donald Glas and other clan chiefs were summoned to Blair Castle in August. Many still believed that the Jacobite cause was not lost. James, himself, was still in Ireland and there was hope of help from Louis XIV of France. A Bond of Association was drawn up between the chiefs. They promised to meet in September and to provide protection and assistance to anyone of their cause.

Donald Glas signed the bond for the MacGregors and then returned home with Rob to assess their domestic situation. During their absence the farm had suffered badly. The crops had failed and, in order to find food and supplies for his family, it was necessary for Donald Glas to do a spot of reiving. However, during a raid on Kilmaronock, Donald was captured and taken to Stirling Castle, and then, three months later, to Edinburgh. Although the laird of Kilmaronock agreed to drop the charges, the Privy Council was not prepared to let a well-known Jacobite rebel go free. Donald was charged with treason, and was to be held prisoner for two further years.

In his father's enforced absence Rob's older brother Iain led the clan. During a hard winter many clans, including the MacGregors, robbed neighbouring farms in order to survive.

Castle Grant.

Unfortunately for the Jacobites, their troubles did not end there. A Jacobite force, led by Major General Thomas Buchan and Colonel Cannon, was summoned in April 1690 and Iain, as his father's representative, joined them. Rob did not go this time. The family needed a strong leader at home and so Rob remained as acting chief.

Buchan's forces of about 800 were camped at Cromdale, near Grantown on Spey. At nearby Castle Grant, a government army led by Sir Thomas Livingstone learned of the Jacobites' position and acted quickly. He led his troops on an enforced march and attacked at dawn. The Jacobites – unprepared and still half-asleep – were routed with the loss of 300 men. This brought the 1690 Rising in Scotland to an end.

James VII had sent word that he could raise men in Ireland. Once he had won there, he would bring an army to Scotland and prepare for an invasion of England. William of Orange immediately left for Ireland, and the two armies met at the Battle of Boyne. The Jacobites were easily defeated and James had no choice but to return to exile in France.

After the 1690 rising, life for Rob Roy and his family continued to be difficult. There was little hope that his father Donald Glas would be released. For some time, due to their involvement at Killiecrankie and Cromdale, both Iain and Rob were unable to work as cattle dealers. They had to resort to reiving and thievery to provide basic necessities such as grain.

Rather than steal cattle, however, Iain formed the 'Lennox Watch' and agreed to protect the lands of the Lennox in return for blackmail. Rob helped him and their success brought Rob to the attention of the Campbell Earl of Breadalbane. Breadalbane had had his own cattle lifted by the MacRaes of Kintail, and asked Rob to recover the beasts. Rob successfully restored Breadalbane's cattle, and this earned him both money and a good reputation. Other local magnates, such as Montrose and Kilmanan, soon got Rob to provide protection for their own cattle.

Meanwhile, William of Orange was successfully alienating many of his subjects, and it soon became clear that he was little better than the Stewart kings. Although the 1689-90 rising had failed, the Jacobites were still plotting and scheming; the episcopalians resented the establishment of the presbyterian church, and many were themselves now being persecuted; the Cameronians were angry as William disregarded parts of the Covenant; and there were also many disappointed nobles and politicians, who felt that they had been deprived of the high office they merited – at least in their own eyes.

Sadly for James VII his campaign to recover his crown came to nothing and how he must have come to rue his panicked flight to France in 1689. Louis XIV of France did not want to waste money when Jacobite support and success was uncertain.

Nevertheless, support for the Jacobite cause did continue. Many also forgot their dislike or distrust of James when faced with the aftermath of the Massacre of Glencoe.

This sent shockwaves through the Highlands and Lowlands, and must have concerned the MacGregors – who were in a similar position to the MacDonalds of Glencoe.

In 1691 William of Orange had appointed Sir John Dalrymple, Master of Stair, as Joint Secretary of State in Edinburgh. Dalrymple instructed Breadalbane to meet with the clan chiefs to discuss, persuade or bribe them to lay down their arms and take the Oath of Allegiance.

The meeting was held at the ruined old castle of Achallader (which had been burnt by the MacGregors in 1603). Donald Glas was still in prison and neither Iain nor Rob attended for the MacGregors.

It was agreed that there would be an armistice until October, but if James VII returned with support then the truce would be over. William of Orange then proclaimed that he would pardon everyone who took the Oath of Allegiance before 1 January 1692. This notice was posted throughout markets in Scotland and, although time was short, messengers were sent to James asking him to release the chiefs from their promise to him: they would not sign unless he freed them from their obligations. James delayed in his response to the chiefs' request, which did not help his subjects.

Donald Glas, in prison in Edinburgh, refused to consider signing William's Oath. However, his wife Margaret then died and he agreed to sign the Oath in return for his freedom.

Although the Privy Council accepted the oath, they refused to release him until he had paid the cost of his imprisonment, some 10,000 merks in all. Government troops seized the MacGregor rents, infuriating Rob. Rob decided to seek some recompense, and find money to pay his father's ransom. He chose to raid the lands of Sir Alexander Livingstone of Bedlormie, who held property around Kippen. This escapade became known as 'the Hership of Kippen'.

Kippen.

The local men of Kippen were understandably upset when they learnt of Rob's intentions. They armed themselves in an attempt to stop his men from lifting their cattle and plundering their property. Rob had no wish to get involved in a battle as any deaths would likely get him into serious trouble. Consequently the MacGregors held off fighting for as long as possible. Eventually they had no choice but to use their swords against men armed only with scythes and flails. Livingstone's drover was killed and others were wounded, much to Rob's irritation.

When he went to 'discuss' events with the men of Kippen, they had already, perhaps not surprisingly, fled the village. Rob regarded as cowardliness in abandoning their homes and beasts, and he took a cow from every byre to add to those he had already acquired from Livingstone.

Despite this action the Privy Council still released Donald Glas and he returned to Glengyle, but his imprisonment and the death of his wife had left him a broken man.

John Dalrymple, Master of Stair, was becoming increasingly frustrated at the time it was taking for the chiefs to take the Oath of Allegiance. In December 1691 Duncan

Menzies of Forneth returned to Edinburgh with a release for the chiefs from James VII. However, time was running out as the oath had to be taken by 31 December. After much hesitation, and with differing degrees of reluctance, nearly all the chiefs took it. MacLean of Duart and MacDonald of Glengarry refused, but they were too powerful to be singled out by the government for punishment.

MacIain of Glencoe, chief of a small branch of the once large and powerful MacDonalds, was a more suitable target to be made an example. In all truth MacIain intended to take the oath, but went to Fort William, arriving there on 31 December which might have been all right. Unfortunately, Colonel Hill, governor of the garrison, was not permitted to accept the oath, so MacIain then had to set off for Inveraray. He did not arrive there until 2 January: his journey was hampered by bad weather. The oath was accepted on 6 January, some six days late. The further delay was said to have been due to Campbell of Ardkinglas, the sheriff, suffering from his overindulgence in the New Year celebrations. When news arrived at Edinburgh MacIain's oath was rejected, although as far as the MacDonalds of Glencoe knew there was no problem.

The MacDonalds of Glencoe were an ideal target for retribution: they were a small and powerless clan; they lived in an area from which there was no easy escape; they were staunch supporters of James VII; and they were reputedly a lawless lot.

It was organised by John Dalrymple, Master of Stair, although it is likely that Breadalbane was aware of the plan. Orders were passed to Sir Thomas Livingstone, Commander-in-Chief in Scotland, but before they went down the line of command, they were signed by William of Orange. Colonel Hill's orders, however, were clear: no mercy was to be shown to the MacDonalds of Glencoe.

On 1 February 1692 the Campbell Earl of Argyll's regiment was moved into Glencoe and quartered on the

Glencoe.

MacDonalds. The MacDonalds had not paid their taxes, and so could not refuse to give the government troops hospitality.

Captain Robert Campbell of Glenlyon was in charge. He was a 60-year-old alcoholic and had been ruined – at least partly – by the MacDonalds of Glencoe plundering his lands. He was also the brother of Rob Roy's mother, Margaret Campbell. His orders were that all men of the clan, who were under 70 years of age, were to be slain.

At dawn on 13 February the massacre began. MacIain, his wife, two of his sons and a number of the clan, about 38 in total, were killed by government troops. Nevertheless, the massacre was badly executed – probably deliberately so and the Campbells may have warned their intended victims. Many of the MacDonalds escaped from the glen, and found refuge with the Stewarts of Appin to the south and west of Glencoe, although others died in the snow of the passes.

The consequences of the massacre were not as anticipated by Dalrymple and the government. Ironically they had handed the Jacobites a propaganda victory, and a storm of criticism rose, directed at all those involved, from the troops on the ground right up to William of Orange. Criticism was even levelled from the Lowlands, where normally Highlanders were scorned and feared. The cruel and treacherous act, far from cowing the Highlands, led to increased support for the Jacobites.

Rob continued to provide protection in return for blackmail and cattle trading. He also continued, however, to thieve beasts from areas outside his 'protection'. His attentions were particularly turned on the Murray Marquis of Atholl, and he raided his lands in Strathearn. In Rob's defence, although he had no conscience about helping himself to others people's beasts, he was also known to help others in less fortunate circumstances. He would provide meat or meal or replacement animals.

Rob was betrothed to Helen Mary (she was called Mary) MacGregor of Comer, his cousin. Mary is said to have been a high-spirited lass – indeed, some have blamed her for inciting Rob to much of his mischief. It seems unlikely, however, that Rob needed any such incitement.

It is possible that Iain, his older brother, returned to Glengyle at this time in order to take over his father's responsibilities. Rob and Mary were married at Corryarklet, between Loch Lomond and Loch Katrine, on 1 January 1693 – as recorded in the Buchanan parish register.

In February the chief of the MacGregors died without any legitimate heir. Although he was chief in name, he had been rather weak, and it was Donald Glas, Rob's father, who had proved a more inspiring leader. The position of chief was now taken up by Archibald MacGregor of Kilmanan, captain of Glenstrae.

In the August the proscription of the clan was reintroduced, although there does not appear to be any obvious reason for this. The chiefs had all been pardoned, even MacDonald of Glencoe, and the MacGregors had not been involved in any rebellion since Killiecrankie and Cromdale. It is possible that the Marquis of Atholl, whose lands Rob had raided, may have been behind the proscription. Rob changed his name to Campbell, that of his mother, so that he could travel freely and conduct business.

Rob continued to run and increase the extent of the Lennox Watch. He trained his men well and had proved himself reliable. His protection, although it cost money, meant that men could rear and market their cattle without fear of loss.

In 1695 Rob signed a bond with Atholl, and agreed to stop raiding his lands. Rob was being ever the more closely pursued, and he must have had other things on his mind. Mary gave birth to James, known as James Mor, their first son, and for a time things appeared to have settled down.

Rob was arrested, however, while at market in Glasgow. On 19 December 1695 the Privy Council ordered Rob to be sent to Flanders. Rob Roy was nothing if not resourceful. He contrived to escape, possibly with the help of his prison guards who were Highlanders like himself, and was home by the end of the year.

Over the next four years Rob and his family, along with the rest of Scotland, had to endure the time known as 'The Hungry Years'. There were four harvest failures in a row due to poor summer weather, and there was also an outbreak of cattle disease, which Rob must have sorely felt. Suffering was widespread and many people died.

Around the same time an intriguing proposal occupied many people in Scotland: the Darien Scheme. The enterprise began in 1695 when the Scottish Parliament passed an Act for the establishment of a 'company of Scotland trading to Africa and the Indies'. There was some vague support from William of Orange, although English merchants were not keen on the plan.

The Scots modelled the new company 'The Company of Scotland' on the very successful English East India Company, granting it similar privileges. It was to be a joint enterprise with the English. Half the capital was to be raised in London, and the company was to be managed from London. Enthusiasm was high initially and £300 000 was raised in two weeks.

Support in England, however, evaporated when the English House of Commons threatened to impeach the directors: many English merchants saw the Scottish company as a threat to their economic interests. The East India Company was to keep its monopoly, and the Scottish company was left to struggle on without official support. William was now actively hostile, blocking the borrowing of money and the purchasing of ships.

This opposition by William and the English encouraged the Scots into a frenzy of fund raising, and they managed to raise capital of £400 000. On 12 July 1698 three ships and two smaller vessels set sail from Leith, for Darien on the isthmus of Panama.

The ships arrived on 3 November at a sheltered spot called Acla, which was renamed Caledonia, and the colonists built a small settlement, called New Edinburgh and Fort St Andrew.

The scheme was ill conceived, badly planned, and poorly implemented. The Scots found themselves between the English in Jamaica to the north, and the Spanish to the south. The English were not allowed to trade with the Scots – William of Orange did not wish to antagonise the Spanish – while the Spanish, who claimed the area, prepared to attack the new settlement.

Things got worse: supplies were low, desertions and disease were common, and English and Spanish hostility was growing.

In June the colonists abandoned the settlement, and despite a second expedition, the whole scheme was doomed. None of the ships returned to Leith.

Scotland had lost 2000 people and upwards of £200 000, and much anger was directed against William of Orange and the English, some translating to support for the Jacobites. The scheme left Scotland in serious economic difficulties, not helped by the poor harvests. Scottish troops were also being raised to fight in William's wars with the French, and this led to further resentment.

Meanwhile Rob and Mary had managed to survive the ill years and avoid any involvement in the Darien scheme. The early years of the 18th century, however, were no less eventful. Rob's brother, Iain, died as a result of the famine and Iain's son, Gregor, was now heir to Glengyle. In 1701 Archibald Kilmanan signed over the township of Knockyle near Rowardennan, by Loch Lomond to Rob. This additional property meant that he now had fair amount of land: he was Rob Roy MacGregor of Inversnaid and Craigrostan.

Loch Lomond from Rowardennan.

Family Tree of Kings of Scots, England and Britain (1567-1830)

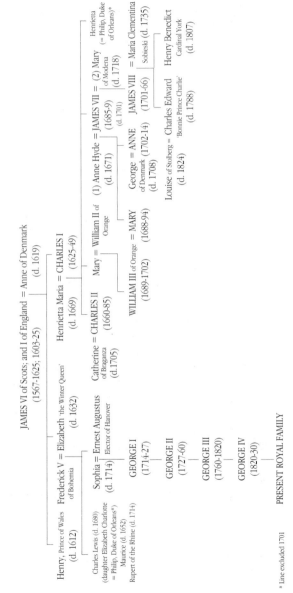

JAMES VI of Scots; and I of England = Anne of Denmark
(1567-1625; 1603-25) | (d. 1619)

Henry, Prince of Wales
(d. 1612)

Frederick V = Elizabeth 'the Winter Queen'
of Bohemia | (d. 1632)

Charles Lewis (d. 1680)
(daughter Elizabeth Charlotte
= Philip, Duke of Orleans*)
Maurice (d. 1652)
Rupert of the Rhine (d. 1714)

Sophia = Ernest Augustus
(d. 1714) | Elector of Hanover

GEORGE I
(1714-27)

GEORGE II
(1727-60)

GEORGE III
(1760-1820)

GEORGE IV
(1820-30)

PRESENT ROYAL FAMILY

Henrietta Maria = CHARLES I
(d. 1669) | (1625-49)

Catherine = CHARLES II
of Braganza | (1660-85)
(d.1705)

Mary = William II of
Orange

WILLIAM III of Orange = MARY
(1689-1702) | (1688-94)

(1) Anne Hyde = JAMES VII = (2) Mary
(d. 1671) | (1685-9) | of Modena
| (d. 1701) | (d. 1718)

George = ANNE
of Denmark | (1702-14)
(d. 1708)

JAMES VIII = Maria Clementina
(1701-66) | Sobieski (d. 1735)

Louise of Stolberg = Charles Edward
(d. 1824) | 'Bonnie Prince Charlie'
| (d. 1788)

Henry Benedict
Cardinal York
(d. 1807)

Henrietta
(= Philip, Duke
of Orleans)*

* Line excluded 1701

4-Rebel and Outlaw 1701-16
Bankruptcy, reiving and rebellions

During the next few years Rob continued to consolidate his reputation, both as an effective cattle drover and as captain of the Lennox Watch. His reputation as an excellent swordsman also grew, enhanced by the large number of duels he fought and won. Rob and Mary had five sons – James Mor or Roy (1695), Coll (1698), Duncan (1704), Ranald (1706) and Robin Oig (1716) – who grew into manhood, although it is likely that there were others who did not survive.

Donald Glas died in 1702 and, as his heir Gregor was still only a boy of 13, Rob was regarded by many as the acting chief of the clan. Rob's family also refused to recognise Iain of Glencarnaig as Kilmanan's successor. Iain was known to like his drink, which could only make him a weak leader.

James VII had died in exile the previous year, and his son, another James Edward, was still only a young boy. William of Orange, himself, died in 1702 when his horse stumbled over a molehill and he was thrown: he had no legitimate children. The throne then passed to his sister-in-law, Anne. She was James VII's daughter, Mary's sister, and therefore a Stewart. Although Anne was happily married and had many children, none of them survived into adulthood. It became clear that it was likely she would also have no heir. George, Elector of Hanover, was put forwards as the next king, although his relation to Anne was more distant. Jacobite hopes continued with James Edward, who became known as 'the Old Pretender' and was recognised as James VIII and III, at least by his supporters.

Anne was not really interested in her northern kingdom, and the Scottish administration was run by James Douglas,

Duke of Queensberry. Anne's reign was dominated by the debate in society about the possible union of the parliaments of Scotland and England.

Relations between the two countries were not at their best at the beginning of the 18th century. For some, particularly the Jacobites, the union of parliaments was abhorrent and they felt that Scotland was being subsumed into its old enemy. In England there was some support for a union in order to abolish the independent Scottish parliament and reduce the possibility of disputes over foreign policy and wars. The 'awkwardness' of the Scottish parliament was demonstrated by the reluctance to become involved in the war against France (the French had, after all, been allies in past centuries) in the War of the Spanish Succession. The Scots passed an Act Against Peace and War in 1703 and an Act of Security in 1704 which questioned the acceptability of the succession of George Elector of Hanover. The English passed the Alien Act in 1705 which gave the Scots ten months to repeal the Act of Security and enter negotiations for union or else they would lose the right to English citizenship and duty-free trade.

After much bartering and bribery, the Union of Parliaments was agreed in 1707, due in a large part to the machinations of the Campbell 2nd Duke of Argyll among others (including the Erskine 6th Earl of Mar). It was to be a union of incorporation. Scotland would keep its church and legal system, but there was be one parliament, one monarch, one flag, one coinage, and one system of weights and measures. Scottish merchants were allowed free access to English colonies which had been denied by an act of the English parliament in 1661. The financial benefits for some were clear. Others were less sure, and there were riots against the union in Edinburgh, Dumfries and Glasgow.

Although national political events may have had some bearing on Rob's opinions, his life continued much as before. This must have been a bright period as things were

*James Graham, Marquis of Montrose and
1st Duke of Montrose (unknown artist).*

going well. His ability and reputation as a successful cattle dealer were further enhanced, and brought him to the attention of James Graham, Marquis of Montrose, who employed him to administer his beasts at market. His dealings with Montrose involved large amounts of money and risk, but their arrangements were mutually beneficial. As Rob often took the stock to England to sell, the Alien Act affected his and Montrose's profits. Many lost heavily although Rob survived. He also did particularly well when the Alien Act was repealed, as he was able to sell stock which he had bought for a greatly reduced price in Scotland at a greatly increased price in England. As a Jacobite, however, he was certainly opposed to the Hanoverian succession in particular, and probably the Union of 1707 in general.

As with many other clans, the MacGregors were opposed to any scheme which was supported by, and benefited, the Campbells of Argyll. Argyll was made a Knight of the Garter as well as being given the Earldom of Greenwich. Others also benefited including Montrose, himself, who was raised to a Duke; Queensberry who was made Duke of Dover and Marquis of Beverley; and the Earl of Mar was promoted to Secretary of State and Privy Councillor. Mar was to feature prominently in the later years.

In 1708 hopes were raised that there might be a Jacobite rising led by James VIII and III, 'the Old Pretender'. There was some support from Louis XIV of France and many of the clans supported the plan, at least in theory. Rob and his nephew were involved in the preparations although, wisely, they did so in secret.

Louis provided a small fleet and his best naval commander, and James departed from Dunkirk in March 1708. The plan was to sail to the Firth of Forth, land at Leith and besiege Edinburgh. At the same time the Jacobites would rise in the north. The voyage, however, was a rough one and James was not a good sailor. Bad weather and the presence of a number of English warships prevented the French ships from putting ashore. They then sailed further north before returning to France by 7 April 1708. The attempted rising was over before it had even begun, and James had not even put his foot on Scottish soil. Many regard this as an opportunity missed by the Jacobites, but it is difficult to know how much support they could have raised with Anne, who was a Stewart, still on the throne.

Rob returned to his family and continued to prosper. He was now in his 30s, and bought more property. And he was trusted by men of wealth and power, both Lowlander and Highlander. Much of his time was spent negotiating deals and cattle trading, as well as involving himself in the Jacobite cause. Rob had so many contracts that he needed to employ other men to carry out some of the work.

One of those he trusted most was his chief drover, Duncan MacDonald, who ran his nephew's farm at Monachyle Tuarach, near Loch Doine, at Balquhidder. In the summer of 1711 Rob borrowed £1000 sterling from the Duke of Montrose and other clients. This was a huge sum of money in the 18th century, and was needed to purchase and prepare cattle for the markets in the following year. In April of 1712 he sent MacDonald, and some other men, with letters of credit to bring in the cattle. MacDonald, however, ran off with the money – or so it seems.

The arrangement with Montrose meant that Rob took responsibility for the theft – the most likely outcome was that he would be bankrupted. Little is known about MacDonald's motives: he may have stolen the money himself or perhaps he was working with others. What is known is that he was never found despite Rob's desperate attempts – it has been suggested that MacDonald was in fact innocent, and was murdered and robbed by parties unknown, although this would obviously benefit Montrose.

Montrose was originally told that the money and Rob Roy were both gone: although Rob was actually searching high and low for news of MacDonald. Instead of giving Rob the benefit of the doubt, Montrose decided that Rob was involved in the scheme. Rob tried to pay back as much money as possible but Montrose took out a court order declaring Rob bankrupt. Advertisements were placed in the Edinburgh *Evening Courant* proclaiming Rob a thief and encouraging anyone to turn him over to the authorities in return for a reward. Montrose's behaviour seems a bit odd: either he saw an opportunity to finally get revenge on Rob or perhaps he was even involved in stealing the money himself.

Rob was summoned to appear for trial but, probably wisely, did not go. He knew he would have been summarily imprisoned as he could not pay back the money. He offered to compensate Montrose through Graham of Killearn,

Montrose's factor. Montrose would hear none of it, and wanted Rob's lands of Craigrostan. Rob was faced with the loss of his freedom or the loss of his property, or probably both. Knowing what effect such a loss would have on his MacGregor clansmen and his family, Rob chose neither and instead headed north. On 3 October 1712 Rob was declared an outlaw and a warrant issued for his arrest.

Rob appealed for help from Atholl, who did not respond: perhaps because Rob had raided his lands in the past. Nevertheless Rob managed to escape arrest but Montrose turned his anger on a more vulnerable target: Rob's wife and family. He instructed Graham of Killearn to take troops, seize Craigrostan, and evict Mary and Rob's children.

In March 1713 troops carried out his orders without mercy. It is said that Mary was raped and branded, and she fled to Portnellan where she was given refuge by her kin. Whether Montrose sanctioned what was done that day is not known, perhaps he derived some satisfaction from acquiring Craigrostan. It may have appeared that his position was now secure, but his orders and the behaviour of his men could only result in Rob seeking revenge and wreaking havoc with Montrose's property – which of course Rob duly did. It no longer mattered: Rob was an outlaw, his wife and family had been cruelly mistreated, and his land had been seized. He had been branded as an outlaw so he might as well act like one.

Rob continued to move around the Highlands, successfully avoiding capture and taking refuge where possible. He was given shelter at the Campbell Earl of Breadalbane's stronghold of Finlarig. Breadalbane leased Rob a property at Auchinchisallen in Glen Dochart. Breadalbane may have been involved in Jacobite plotting, but his motive for helping Rob seems to have had more to do with his dislike of Montrose. Perhaps he felt having a man of Rob Roy's

Glen Dochart.

skill and knowledge working with him could do him no harm.

Rob moved his family to Auchinchisallen and returned to his earlier occupation of lifting beasts and extracting blackmail. He gathered a band of trusted men, based around Loch Katrine, and concentrated his attention on Montrose. He demanded money, no doubt with menaces, from Montrose's tenants in the Lennox and Menteith. Just to keep things all above board, he provided the tenants with a receipt for the full amount taken.

At the same time Rob was prepared to help others, although Montrose unwillingly provided the money, food and livestock. He lent money and food to those who were in dire straits. A widow from Balfron had her rent increased to £20 Scots by Montrose. She could not afford this and was faced with eviction. Rob went to the woman and gave her the required amount. When the bailiffs arrived she was able to pay her rent and got a receipt in return. On their way back, the bailiffs were confronted by a band of Rob's men and the £20 Scots retrieved. Again a receipt was issued by Rob Roy which was to be returned to Montrose.

Queen Anne's death in 1714 brought more problems. George, Elector of Hanover, was reluctant to leave Germany but was proclaimed king in London. Many Scots were outraged. He spoke little English, knew nothing of Scotland, and never visited his northern kingdom. The expected benefits from the union of 1707 had not yet materialised, and there had been several bad harvests. Not all of this was, by any means, the government's fault but it resulted in unrest and disenchantment. It was a fine opportunity for the Jacobites and those who hated the Union.

This time the rising was fermented in Scotland, and Rob Roy MacGregor had a large part to play in the preparations – as mentioned before: he now had little to lose. With his cattle-dealing connections, he was a useful liaison between the chiefs and nobles such as Breadalbane. There had been

John Erskine, 6th Earl of Mar (G. Kneller).

the whiff of rebellion during the summer of 1714, especially at cattle markets and other gatherings. Montrose was aware of the discontent and sent troops to Crieff to quell any trouble before it got going.

John Erskine, 6th Earl of Mar, was the leader of the rising when it came in 1715. He had been Secretary of State for Scotland under Anne but he was deprived of office by George. It was due to this more than any other motive that he discovered his Jacobite tendency. Indeed, Mar had been a staunch supporter of the Union.

This habit of changing sides when it suited earned him the nickname of 'Bobbing John'. It must have seemed a Godsend to the Jacobites at the time. Mar was a well-known character who had wielded power; he was also a Lowlander and a protestant. He was also a politician rather than a solider.

The standard was raised at Braemar on 19 September 1715 and James VIII proclaimed King of Scots. With his usual mixture of bad luck and poor judgement, James VIII was on the other side of Europe. To complicate things further Louis XIV of France, who might have aided them, had just died.

The support of the Highland chiefs was not as certain as it might have been. More than a few could not trust Mar and questioned his leadership abilities. They also feared the reputation and power of the Campbells in general and John Campbell, 2nd Duke of Argyll, in particular who was a staunch Hanoverian. Argyll was also a soldier.

Argyll, however, could only raise a small army, partly made up of Hessian mercenaries from Germany, who he neither liked nor trusted. He mustered his force at Stirling but was not very confident: Argyll thought nine out of ten Scots would support the rising because of the unpopularity of King George.

Mar raise an army of around 12 000 men. From Braemar he struck out in three directions. He sent Gordon of Auchintoul westwards to capture Fort William and hold the west Highlands. The Master of Caithness was sent to take Fife; and Mar led the main army south to Perth. Mackintosh of Borlum seized Inverness. In the west the MacDonalds, Camerons, MacLeans, MacDougalls, Stewarts – and the MacGregors, led by Rob's nephew Gregor MacGregor (or Graham) of Glengyle, also known as 'Black Knee' – prepared for battle.

Rob Roy had a plan to attack the castle at Dumbarton which was in a strategic position controlling the Clyde and routes into the Highlands. It was vulnerable as it was poorly defended, but Mar felt this move would only attract attention from Government forces and he wanted to keep the coast clear for the eventual arrival of James VIII.

Instead Rob was entrusted with carrying orders and money to Breadalbane and Gordon of Auchintoul. In September Mar ordered all the boats on Loch Lomond to

Loch Lomond.

be seized and in October there was a plan to threaten the Lowlands from Strathfillan.

James VIII still did not arrive in Scotland, and this continued delay caused problems for Mar and the Jacobite leadership. It was decided that Mackintosh of Borlum would cross the Firth of Forth from Fife – which was firmly in Jacobite hands – to the East Lothian coast. Mar would advance west of Stirling, and Rob was needed to guide Mar past the Fords of Frew. Some reckon Mar should have attacked Stirling and ravaged Argyll, but he lacked military experience. Despite having such a large number of troops he continued to wait for James.

Mackintosh landed and marched on Haddington, which he duly took. Next day his force headed for Edinburgh. Argyll, aware of Mackintosh's plans and under no immediate threat from Mar, arrived back from Stirling and refortified the capital. Mackintosh decided that he could not take Edinburgh so advanced on the port of Leith. Argyll, confident that Edinburgh was now safe, quickly returned to Stirling.

Mar continued to delay at Perth but in November finally decided to advance south. Word had come of the arrival of English warships in the Clyde. It was feared that troops would be landed, and would advance into the Highlands and outflank Mar's army. Rob Roy was to go to Flanders Moss and cross the Forth at the Fords of Frew in advance of the main party – it was the only possible crossing place for Argyll's cavalry.

When he arrived there he found government dragoons holding the south side of the river, and sent word to Mar. Rob knew that there were crossings further to the west and he could have led the Jacobites safely to Stirling and attacked Argyll from the rear. Mar would have none of it, and had already reached Dunblane. He decided to confront Argyll in an open battle, and sent for Rob Roy and the MacGregors. Gordon of Auchintoul was to bring troops from the west and meet with Mar at Tullibardine. Mar heavily outnumbered Argyll but chose to allow Argyll to march to Sheriffmuir. This open ground was probably more suited to Argyll than Mar.

The two armies met on 13 November at Sheriffmuir. The right flank of the Jacobites routed the left side of the Hanoverian troops, while Argyll and his dragoons attacked the Jacobite right flank and drove them back. But, as the hours passed, no clear victory emerged, and a strange stalemate emerged with the centre of both armies reluctant to fight. Neither side wished to pursue the battle and both eventually withdrew.

Rob and his men took no part in the fighting and because of this some have labelled him a coward. This is somewhat harsh: Rob and his men only arrived at Sheriffmuir as the two armies were withdrawing. Rob Roy, it appears, was urged to attack but the MacGregors had already marched many miles that day and must have been tired. Rob Roy may also have decided that it was not worth risking his own men at this stage. He was reputed to say: 'If they cannot do it without me, they cannot do it with me!'. That much is most likely true. He used his men to cover the Jacobite army while it regrouped.

Rob was also accused of plundering, and of this he was more than likely guilty. Plundering was an accepted part of warfare at this time, and was the only reason many got involved.

As the next morning dawned it became clear that the Jacobites had been left in command of the field: Argyll's forces had retired to Stirling during the night. Mar claimed victory, but unwisely did not press home the advantage. Argyll remained at Stirling with his army.

Mar dithered somewhat, and ordered his forces back to Perth to reorganise – and wait the arrival of James VIII. This proved to be a mistake. The Highlanders had been away from home for some months, and only fought because of loyalty to their chiefs, and no doubt in some cases the thought of loot. Mar had proved himself a less than decisive leader, and many clansmen melted away back to their families and homes.

The indecisive victory, if victory it was, was certainly bad propaganda. The French and Spanish were reluctant to support a failing cause. More bad news came from

England. A Jacobite army of Lowlanders and some Highlanders, led by Macintosh of Borlum, had been defeated at Preston on 14 November. Inverness fell to a Hanoverian force led by Simon Fraser of Lovat and, in December, 6 000 Dutch troops arrived from the continent to reinforce the Hanoverian army. James VIII did not arrive at Aberdeen until Christmas Eve.

In early December Mar had given Rob orders to take his men to the Lennox and Menteith and raid Montrose's lands, which it must be assumed he readily agreed to do. Montrose, on the other hand, offered to return Craigrostan to Rob if he could supply evidence that Argyll had been involved in plotting with the Jacobites. On the face of it this seems a fanciful claim. When Rob refused Montrose issued orders to seize Rob, but Montrose's men failed to capture him.

When news of James's arrival came Mar sent Rob and his men, under 'Black Knee' MacGregor of Glengyle, to Falkland Palace in Fife. Part of Perthshire, Fife and Angus were still held by the Jacobites. Based at Falkland, Rob undertook a little light plundering until January. When it

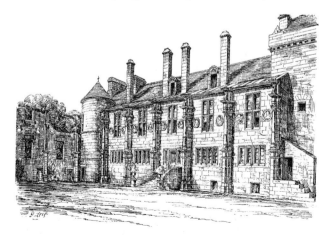

Falkland Palace.

appeared that a Hanoverian force would seize Balgonie Tower, Rob garrisoned the castle with 200 men.

James VIII travelled to Scone and set up court at the palace, but he had arrived too late and the rising was in its death throes. Men continued to desert, and those who remained were cold, hungry and increasingly dispirited. Argyll now had the measure of Mar, and advanced to Perth, and Mar and James withdrew north to Montrose. From there the Jacobite army was sent to Aberdeen, while Mar and James VIII boarded ship and fled back to France. Rob and his men marched to Aberdeenshire, then went to join the MacDonalds in Strathspey.

Parliament passed an act accusing anyone involved in the Battle of Sheriffmuir of treason – unless they surrendered by June 1716. Rob Roy appeared among the 49 named. Having returned to Stirlingshire, Rob continued to raid but he received word that his house at Auchinchisallen was to be burnt. Rob was in a vulnerable position: clearly government troops would continue to pursue him and harass his family until he surrendered.

Ironically, given the long term ill-feeling and ill-will

Loch Katrine.

between the MacGregors and the Campbells, and his support of the Hanoverians, it was to the Campbell Duke of Argyll that Rob turned. After Sheriffmuir Argyll lost favour with the authorities. Indeed some, including Montrose, had tried to accuse Argyll of secretly supporting the Jacobites – which seems preposterous under the circumstances. It is also true that Rob remained loyal to the Duke even when betraying him would have greatly benefited him.

In June Rob and his men travelled to Inveraray and there, technically at least, surrendered. In order to meet the terms of the act, they handed in a collection of rusty old guns and swords. Argyll allowed Rob to build a house at Glen Shira – although Mary and the children stayed at Loch Katrine.

5 - Reconciliation 1716-35

Escape and peace.

Rob continued to thoroughly antagonise Montrose and Graham of Killearn. In November Killearn was busy collecting Montrose's rents, and he was lodged in an inn at Chapelarroch, near Aberfoyle. On the 20th of the month Rob stole to the inn, and unexpectedly broke in on Killearn. He searched the building for money, took what he could find and, as was his custom, wrote out a receipt for Montrose.

Rob made sure that Killearn knew that the rent money would in part repay the cost of the burning of Rob's house at Craigrostan and the loss of his beasts. Rob then seized Killearn and took him to Portnellan by the north shore of Loch Katrine. Killearn was 'persuaded' to write a letter to Montrose which explained Rob's demands for compensation for the burning of Craigrostan and Auchinchisallen. Rob must have wanted to revenge himself on Killearn for the cruel attack on his wife and house. But in the end he let Killearn go. Keeping him prisoner would not resolve the situation, and harming or killing him would simply make things worse.

Montrose must have been furious, and redoubled and trebled his efforts to have Rob stopped and captured. Spurred on by Rob's non-stop raiding of this lands, he sought help from the government. Rob's reputation as an outlaw was growing, and many, even powerful men such as Sir Adam Cockburn of Ormiston, Lord Justice Clerk, were now frightened to travel in this area of Scotland unless accompanied by a strong bodyguard of armed men.

Montrose's pleas were answered. The Independent Companies of Militia were ordered to scour the area to apprehend Rob. These militia were mostly Campbell troops which was somewhat ironic given that the Duke of Argyll had offered Rob protection at Glen Shira. Of course, this may explain why they had no success.

Montrose took matters into his own hands. In March 1717 he obtained letters of Fire and Sword as well as a commission to gather a force to seize Rob. An act had been passed which pardoned those who had been involved in the 1715 Jacobite rising – except those of the name MacGregor that is.

Rob managed to stay at large through most of April, but Montrose turned up at Balquhidder unexpectedly and

Balquhidder – ruins of the old kirk.

captured him. Montrose took no chances as he knew Rob was extremely resourceful. He had Rob mounted on a horse, with his arms tightly tied, and began the journey back to Stirling with Rob as captive.

When they reached the Forth the river was so swollen that it was necessary to untie Rob's arms. So that there was no chance he could escape, Montrose had him tethered to one of his own men, and then they both mounted his horse. As they were crossing the river, Rob fell from the horse, taking his companion with him. In the confusion he cut the tether and managed to swim away. Montrose could do nothing and Rob evaded his men. This episode certainly enhanced what was becoming Rob's legendary reputation.

It was then the Duke of Atholl who continued the pursuit – Montrose may have had enough. Atholl was one of the most powerful men in Scotland. Although he was resolute in his support of George I, his sons were nevertheless Jacobites. Charles, one of his sons, had fought with Mackintosh of Borlum at the defeat at Preston and had been taken prisoner there. The Duke of Roxburghe, now Secretary of State, offered Atholl a pardon for his son if he could capture Rob Roy MacGregor. Atholl was also one of the landowners who had been on the receiving end of Rob's reiving – Atholl owned much property around Balquhidder.

Atholl wrote to Rob and proposed a meeting at Dunkeld House on 3 June 1717. Rob agreed to attend but only on the guarantee of safe conduct. He probably hoped that Atholl would be prepared to give him a refuge around the Balquhidder area in return for his submission. Atholl's proposal, however, involved betraying Argyll as a Jacobite. Despite the offer, which would have ensured his freedom, Rob again refused. Atholl lost patience, and had Rob arrested, despite the guarantee of safe conduct. Atholl claimed that the safe conduct had been signed by his brother and so was not binding on him, which is an interesting distinction.

Rob was sent to Logierait, north of Dunkeld, and held there. It appears he was not searched very carefully. He had arrived at Dunkeld with some money, perhaps to rent land from Atholl. He now put it to good use and bought plenty of whisky for his guards.

It has been suggested that the guards, or some of Atholl's men, may well have helped Rob. Whatever the truth of it, Rob plied his jailers with drink and entertained them with tales of his escapades. In the late morning one of his servants arrived and Rob was brought out of the castle to speak to him. As he exchanged words with the servant, he suddenly leapt onto a horse and galloped off. There was no pursuit.

This did nothing for Atholl's reputation, while again enhancing Rob's. The ease with which he escaped tends to show that he commanded a wide support and affection from both Atholl's own men and other Jacobites.

Montrose and Atholl were not to have it all their own way, and this time Rob retaliated in a novel way. In June 1717 Rob Roy published a declaration which described the actions of Montrose and Atholl. It was circulated around Scotland to many clan chiefs, and cannot have helped either noble.

Rob remained at large, and continued to move stealthily around Loch Katrine, occasionally surprising government forces and seizing their arms. Montrose had given up the hunt by the end of 1717 and, although Atholl continued for a short time, by 1718 he had also given up.

Montrose's malice was not quite exhausted, though. He continued to pursue his claim to Rob's lands at Inversnaid. Rob's property had been seized by the Commissioners for Confiscated Estates. Montrose bought Inversnaid, which he decided to turn into a barracks for a garrison of government troops (which were led at one time by General

Eilean Donan Castle – see next page.

Wolfe, who is well known for exploits against the French in Quebec). The conversion of his home into a garrison was unlikely to please Rob. During the autumn of 1718, the MacGregors raided, harried and attacked the builders in order to stop, or at least delay, the building work. The barracks, however, was eventually completed towards the end of 1719.

Meanwhile, the great powers were moving, and for a while the Jacobite cause coincided with the interests of Spain. Britain had gone to war with Spain in 1718 and, in 1719 the Spanish and the Irish Duke of Ormonde organised another rising. It was to be two pronged. A small, probably diversionary, rising was started in the Mackenzie country of Kintail in Wester Ross, while the main force, led by Ormonde, was to attack the west of England. As ever, Rob Roy was involved.

In April 1719 two Spanish frigates and a small French ship sailed to Loch Alsh, bringing with them the Mackenzie Earl of Seaforth, the Keith Earl Marischal, the Murray Marquis of Tullibardine, and Mackintosh of Borlum, who although he had been captured at Preston, managed to escape from Newgate Prison. There were also about 300 Spanish troops, who must have drawn the short straw.

The Jacobites garrisoned Eilean Donan Castle, and waited to be joined by the clan chiefs and other Jacobites. Rob Roy arrived north with 40 MacGregors. Lord George Murray, son of Atholl; Clanranald, the chief of Clan Ranald; Cameron of Lochiel; and MacDougall of Lorn joined the gathering at Eilean Donan, but others were less sure. They wanted definite proof, both about the amount of foreign support as well as the present whereabouts of James VIII.

After nearly a month only some 1200 had assembled. The large Spanish attack on England never materialised as a storm scattered and dispersed the fleet – as ever the English had the weather on their side.

General Wightman, the government commander of the Highlands, moved west from Inverness with an army composed of non-Jacobites clans, such as the Munros, Frasers and Sutherlands. English warships captured Eilean Donan Castle and then blew it up with gunpowder. It might have been wiser for the Jacobites to disband and reassemble elsewhere, but they marched into Glen Shiel to confront the government forces approaching from the east.

On 11 June 1719 the two armies met. The Jacobites were far from united with the Highlanders and Spanish at loggerheads. They were, however, in a strong position in the steep-sided glen.

The first fighting took place on the side of *Sgour Ouran*, one of the Five Sisters of Kintail, but it was not conclusive. The next morning the battle resumed; but things went from bad to worse for the Jacobites. General Wightman used mortars and muskets to hold off the Jacobites. Then the Earl of Seaforth was wounded, and his Mackenzie clansmen carried him off the field. This was the turning point of the battle.

Battle of Glenshiel (Tillemans).

Defeat quickly followed and the Jacobites withdrew. The Highlanders disappeared into the mountains, while the unfortunate Spaniards were left to surrender – most however eventually made it back to Spain. Tullibardine, Lord George Murray and the Earl of Seaforth escaped to France. The 3200 foot-high mountain is known as the *Sgurr na Spainteach* – the Peak of the Spaniards.

Rob Roy blew up his store of guns and ammunition, hidden at Kintail, to stop it being seized by government forces. He then travelled back south to Glen Shira. There was no direct evidence that he had been present at Glen Shiel, and there was no immediate reprisal.

In 1720 Rob moved back to Inverlochlarig Beag, near Balquhidder, a property which was still in truth Atholl's. There he went back to his previous occupations: farming, droving, occasional raiding and extracting blackmail.

Rob made fewer raids into Montrose's lands, perhaps age was mellowing him: he was now approaching 50 years old. Montrose no longer had a great deal of political power, and it was now Argyll who was in favour in London. Argyll had used his power reasonably well, and even in the Highlands was uncommonly popular for a Campbell. He kept in touch with Rob, and attempted to disarm the clans rather than repress them completely.

Rob continued to command the Watch which he could summon if needed – although he did so less often. In 1722 some MacIntyres called on his support. They had been evicted for rent arrears from land at Invercarnaig. They were not strong enough to resist and called for help. Rob ambushed Iain Og, the landlord, and his men, and made them swear an oath not to return. Although this event was reported to Atholl, he did not take any direct action against Rob.

At the same time the English writer and spy, Daniel Defoe, (who is better known for *Robinson Crusoe*, which is similarly based on a real character, Alexander Selkirk) wrote

Rob Roy's Statue, Stirling.

a fictional account of Rob's exploits. *Highland Rogue* was published in 1723 and ensured Rob was elevated to hero rather than villain. This enhanced reputation made life easier for Rob and, to some extent, rehabilitated his name.

Atholl died in 1724 and his sons, who had Jacobite sympathies, were not hostile towards Rob. The same year Argyll persuaded Rob to meet with himself and Montrose on neutral territory. It has been suggested the meeting was in London, but there is no actual record of this. Nevertheless, the meeting took place and a truce was agreed between them.

One reason Rob may have agreed to meet with Argyll and Montrose was General Wade. He had been given command of the army and ordered to pacify the Highlands, disarm the clans, receive submission from the chiefs, and build military roads. Argyll and Montrose very likely advised Rob to submit to Wade, sooner rather than later.

Montrose died in 1724. Rob, although he had agreed to submit, was still excluded from pardon by the king, and consequently was reluctant to do so. The other chiefs were not in a position to refuse, and so eventually sent in their letters of submission. These were not worth the paper on which they were written, but in the meantime they were allowed to carry on their lives without excess harassment from Wade's forces.

Nevertheless, in September 1725 Rob Roy finally sent in his submission. He was no longer a young man, and had reached the relatively mature age of 54. The wording of the letter suggests that it was not written by him. It states that Rob only took part in the 1715 Rising because he was forced to do so, and that he provided Argyll with information about the Jacobites and their plans.

There is very little collaborating evidence to suggest that Rob had been a spy for the Hanoverians, and much to support his loyalty to the Jacobite cause. The wording, however, of the letter damaged Rob's later reputation. Although it is not clear whether this letter resulted in the king's official pardon, the last ten years of Rob's life were peaceful and mostly untroubled by government forces.

In 1730 Rob converted to catholicism. He made his confession to father Alexander Drummond at Drummond Castle, to the south of Crieff. Although he had been brought up in the protestant church he had not been a particularly enthusiastic member of the faith. Also his loyalty to the Jacobite cause may have encouraged his conversion.

By 1734 Rob's health was failing. One of his last visitors was John MacLaren of Invernenty, who was not on best terms with Rob. Although Rob had been bedridden for some weeks, he dressed himself and met his visitor formally. When MacLaren left Rob called for a piper to play *Cha rill me tuille* – 'I shall return no more' – and by the time the tune was finished he had died. This was on 28 December 1734. He was 63, and his exploits were already legendary.

His funeral was held on New Year's Day 1735 and attended by many clansmen. It was held at Balquhidder and his coffin was piped as it was carried down Loch Voil to its final resting place in the burial ground at the old kirk at Balquhidder.

Mary was still alive when Rob died, but it is not known when she finally passed away. She is, however, buried beside him. Rob was survived by his five sons.

Rob Roy's Grave, Balquhidder. Mary, Coll and Robin Oig are also buried here.

6-Postscript: Rob Roy's sons

Although many of Rob Roy's exploits became legendary, he was in truth a resourceful and capable leader, and commanded respect even from his enemies. It is hard to know what would happened if Montrose's £1000 had not gone missing, and it is possible that he would have become for all intents and purposes a successful and legitimate cattle dealer. As it was he lived to a decent age in relative comfort.

Rob appears to have been less involved in the Jacobite cause towards the end of his life, but his sons and clan continued to be active for James VIII. The times were changing, though, and the Scotland in which Rob had been an outlaw was slowly fading away.

Not much needs to be said here about the years after Rob's death, except to explain the deeds of his sons and the general fortunes of the clan.

During the 1720s and 1730s largely ineffective measures, such as the Disarming Act, had been taken to subdue the Highlands. Government garrisons were located at various points, including Inversnaid, and they were connected by miles of military roads.

Discontent rumbled on, but by the 1740s there was general acceptance of the German Georges and the Union. Jacobites continued to scheme, but support was to prove mostly limited to the Highlands – although the clan chiefs would have done better to forget the Stewarts.

James VIII and III had settled in Rome, and in 1719 married Clementina Sobieski, granddaughter of the King of Poland. The 'Young Pretender' Charles Edward, Bonnie Prince Charlie, was born the following year.

In 1745 Charles Edward set out from France with little support and few companions in what proved to be the last

Jacobite rising, the last great adventure of the clans. Prince Charles reached Scotland in July, but was accompanied by only seven companions. He raised the standard at Glenfinnan on 19 August, and the growing army was joined by James Mor, Rob Roy's eldest son, and some 300 men.

The Jacobites set off south, and decided to march on Edinburgh, which they took without any opposition. Charles was welcomed into the city by cheering crowds, and James VIII and III was proclaimed king at the market cross.

The same day a Hanoverian force, led by General Cope, approached Edinburgh but was defeated and routed by the Jacobites at Prestonpans. The MacGregors fought at the battle, and indeed one of their number is said to have slain Colonel Gardiner, one of the most highly placed officers in the government army to be slain.

The Prince's army grew but it consisted almost entirely of Highlanders, and it was decided to invade England, hoping for increased support in the south. They proceeded down the west side of England as far as Derby without any opposition, although support in England was not forthcoming except in Manchester. A council of war was held at Derby on 6 December – 'Black Friday' – and although the Prince wanted to advance on London, the majority opinion was to return to Scotland, and the Jacobites began their withdrawal back north until they were camped near Stirling.

A Hanoverian force, led by General Hawley, advanced into Scotland but was surprised by the Jacobites at the Battle of Falkirk in January 1746. Hawley was quickly defeated and he retreated. Nevertheless the Jacobites could not press their advantage and retreated into the Highlands in front of another advance, this time by a new army led by William Augustus, Duke of Cumberland, later known as the Butcher.

By April the Jacobites were near Inverness, and

Memorial, Culloden Moor.

Cumberland pursued them, marching towards Inverness from Aberdeen. The two armies met on the morning of 16 April 1746 at Culloden Moor. The battle was over in an hour. Hanoverian losses were reckoned at about 350, Jacobite at more than 2000. The MacGregors were at Culloden, although they survived, including James Mor. It was the bloodiest of the Jacobite battles, and the last to be fought on British soil.

The slaughter was to continue after the battle: the Duke of Cumberland, earned his nickname 'Butcher' well. His orders were that there was to be no mercy or quarter. Jacobite wounded and prisoners were shot, bayonetted or clubbed to death. The following day parties were sent to scour the countryside, every house and cottage was searched for wounded, who were then summarily executed, while their shelterers were also punished.

The aftermath of the battle was brutal: fugitives were shot and hanged; houses burned and stock driven off – and the Highland way of life, such as the wearing of plaid, carrying of arms and even the pipes were proscribed. The proscription of the MacGregors was also to continue. The chief of the MacGregors at the time, MacGregor of

Glencarnock, was imprisoned in Edinburgh Castle, and died in 1758.

Rob's sons led as adventurous lives as their father, but they lacked his charisma and some of his resourcefulness. The times were also changing, and the rule of law and order was extended to all parts of Scotland.

James Mor MacGregor, Rob's eldest son, took the surname Drummond. In 1736, with his brother Robin Oig, he was brought to trial accused of the murder of James MacLaren. He was also accused of cattle stealing and escaping from prison. The charges were found not proven.

James fought in both the 1715 and 1745 risings: he was made a major in the latter. With his cousin, MacGregor of Glengyle, he captured and torched the barracks at Inversnaid in 1745. Later the same year, as a captain of the MacGregor Regiment, he was wounded several times at the Battle of Prestonpans. He also fought at Culloden.

In 1752 he was again tried with his brother, Robin Oig – this time for the alleged abduction and forced marriage of the young widow and heiress Jean Kay. James Mor was found guilty and imprisoned in Edinburgh Castle. Luckily for him, he escaped, disguised as a cobbler, with help from his daughter.

James Mor escaped to France and settled in Paris. James was destitute and despite the valuable service he had provided the Jacobites Bonnie Prince Charlie would not help. James was then involved in a plot trying to capture Alan Breck Stewart, who had been implicated in the famous Appin Murder. The idea was to use Stewart to obtain a pardon from the British government. The attempt failed. James Mor was poverty stricken, and died in Paris in 1754. He left a widow and 14 children.

Robin Oig, the 'young', was involved in a quarrel with Robert MacLaren of Invernenty in 1736. MacLaren claimed land which was rented by the MacGregors. Robin, allegedly encouraged by his brothers, shot MacLaren in the back when he was ploughing. He failed to appear for the trial and was outlawed.

He fled to France where he fought at the Battle of Fontenoy. He was wounded and taken prisoner by the French but returned home in 1746. He decided to increase his fortune and marry

Balfron.

Jean Kay, a wealthy and comely young widow. In 1750, with the help of his brothers James Mor and Ranald, he carried her off from Edinbellie, near Balfron. They were married at Rowardennan but she died the following year – it is not clear how willing Jean was in all this. Robin would have inherited her property, but Jean's family were not willing to let the matter rest.

Robin was seized and brought before the High Court of Justiciary in Edinburgh, accused of abduction and forcible marriage. His defence was that the marriage had been entered into at Jean Kay's free will, but this was dismissed. Robin was found guilty and executed.

Coll, however, did much better and prospered as a farmer

although died in 1745. Coll was married in 1721 to Margaret of Coilleitir.

Duncan, who also used the surname Drummond, lived at Strathyre. He was also tried in 1753 for aiding Robin Oig but was found not guilty.

Ranald lived to a great age and died in 1786 at the age of 80. He was married in 1733 to Jean, daughter of MacGregor of Glengyle.

The MacGregors themselves remained outside the law until 1774, when the proscription against them was finally lifted. There was by now no chief. In 1795 a petition, signed by some 826 MacGregors, decided that John Murray (who was in truth a MacGregor) of Lanrick should be their chief. Descended from the MacGregors of Glencarnock, he was a general and served in India.

Sir Evan, his son, was also a general and later Governor of Dominica, and married a daughter of the Duke of Atholl. Sir Evan played a prominent part in the visit of George IV to Scotland in 1822. He and other MacGregors guarded the honours of Scotland, and it was Sir Evan who proposed a toast to George, the 'chief of chiefs', at a royal banquet in Edinburgh.

How Rob Roy would have laughed.

The present chief is Sir Gregor MacGregor of MacGregor, Baronet, 23rd Chief of the MacGregors.

MacGREGOR DESPITE THEM

Places of
Interest

Map 3: Places of Interest

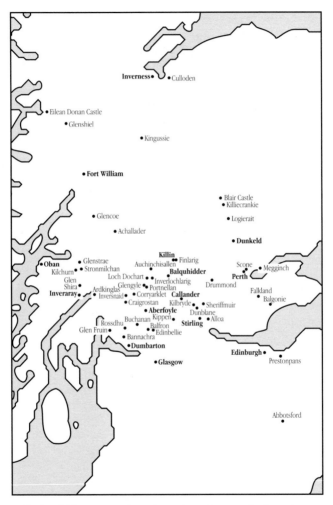

It should be assumed, unless otherwise stated, that places listed are not officially open to the public.

List of Places

Notes

Manned visitor attractions are usually closed at Christmas and New Year.

Price of entry: £ = up to £3.50; ££ = £3.50-£5.00; £££ = £5.00+ Concessions for children, students, OAPs and groups normally apply.

The list on the previous page (page 79) should be used in conjunction with the map (page 78).

Warning

While the information in this book was believed to be correct at time of going to press – and was checked, where possible, with the visitor attractions – opening times and facilities, or other information, may differ from that included. All information should be checked with the visitor attractions before embarking on any journey. Inclusion in the text is no indication whatsoever that a site is open to the public or that it should be visited. Some sites are in difficult and inaccessible locations, while ruinous buildings can be in a dangerous condition. Care should be taken when visiting any site. Inclusion or exclusion of any site should not be considered as a comment or judgement on that site. Locations on the map and national grid references are approximate.

Abbotsford

NT 508343   LR: 73

On B6360, 2 miles W of Melrose, Borders.

Sir Walter Scott, the famous Scottish writer and historian, built Abbotsford as a large castellated mansion with turrets, battlements and corbiestepped gables. Scott collected many historic artefacts, and there is an impressive collection of armour and weapons at the house, including Rob Roy's broadsword, dirk, gun, sporran purse and portrait, and the Marquis of Montrose's sword. Scott wrote the novel *Rob Roy* in 1817. The library has 9000 books.

Open 3rd Monday in Mar-Oct, Mon-Sat & Sun Jun-Sep only, 10.00-17.00; also Sun Mar-May & Oct 14.00-17.00; other dates by appt.
Guided tours. Gift shop. Tearoom. Extensive gardens and grounds. WC. Disabled access by private entrance and WC. Car and coach parking. Group concessions. ££.
Tel: 01896 752043   Fax: 01896 752916
Email: abbotsford@melrose.bordernet.co.uk

Achallader Castle

NN 322442   LR: 50

Off A82, 3.5 miles NE of Bridge of Orchy, Achallader, Argyll.

Not much remains of a 16th-century tower house, which was owned by the Campbells. It was burnt in the first few years of the 17th century by the MacGregors, and in 1689 by Jacobites. The castle was the scene of a conference in 1691 between the Campbell Earl of Breadalbane and Jacobite Highland chiefs, who agreed to an armistice.

Alloa Tower

NTS   NS 889925   LR: 58

Off A907, in Alloa, Clackmannan.

Alloa Tower is a large 14th- or 15th-century keep with
very thick walls,
and still retains a
fine, rare medieval
timber roof. A
later mansion, ad-
joining the castle,
was destroyed by
fire in 1800.

Alloa was given
to Sir Robert Er-
skine,   Great
Chamberlain of
Scotland, in 1360,
and   remained
with his descend-
ants. John Ersk-
ine, 6th Earl of
Mar, was known
as 'Bobbing John'
and led the Jaco-
bites in the 1715 Rising. He was so-called because he
changed sides between the Hanoverians and Jacobites several times. The Rising was a failure partly because of Mar's
poor leadership, and he fled to France where he died, although his son recovered the lands.

Open Easter wknd, then daily May-Sep 13.30-17.30.
Explanatory displays. Collection of portraits of the
Erskine family. WC. Disabled WC and access to ground
floor only. Parking nearby. Group concessions. £.
Tel: 01259 211701

Ardkinglas House

NN 175104   LR: 56

Off A83, 5 miles E of Inveraray, Argyll.

There was a castle here, a property of the Campbells, but it was replaced by Ardkinglas House, built in 1906.

   Alasdair Roy MacGregor was outlawed after the Battle of Glen Fruin in 1603 and captured at Ardkinglas, although he escaped as he was being taken to Inveraray. Campbell of Ardkinglas, as the sheriff, took the Oath of Allegiance from the chief of the MacDonalds of Glencoe at Inveraray in 1692. Campbell was suffering from his overindulgence in the New Year celebrations. When news arrived at Edinburgh the Oath was rejected, and the Massacre of Glencoe resulted.

   The woodland garden has a fine collection of rhododendrons and conifers.

Ardkinglas Woodland Garden open, daily dawn to dusk.
Guided tours. Explanatory displays. Picnic areas. Plant and craft sales and refreshments available from Tree Shop. WC
Tel: 01499 600263   Fax: 01499 600348
Web: www.ardkinglas.com

Argyll's Lodging, Stirling

HS   NS 793938   LR: 57

Off A9, Castle Wynd, Stirling.

Argyll's Lodging is a fine and well-preserved 17th-century town house, and give some idea of how noblemen lived at the time. Gabled blocks with dormer windows surround a courtyard, while one side is enclosed by a wall. Many of the rooms within the lodging have recently been restored and furnished in 17th-century style.

The Lodging was built by Sir William Alexander of Menstrie, but passed to the Campbell Earls of Argyll. The 9th Earl was executed for treason in 1685 after leading a rising against James VII, while the 1st and 2nd Duke of Argyll were involved with Rob Roy and the MacGregors.

Open all year: Apr-Sep, daily 9.00-18.30; Oct-Mar, daily 9.30-17.00; closed Christmas & New Year.
Visitor centre with explanatory displays. Gift shop. WC. Disabled access. Car and coach parking. £ (Joint ticket available with Stirling Castle).
Tel: 01786 461146/450000   Fax: 01786 448194

Auchinchisallen

NN 457275   LR: 51
On A85, 6 miles W of Killin, Auchessan, Stirlingshire.

Parts of a gable and foundations are all that remain of a house. Auchinchisallen was held by Rob Roy from 1713. It was destroyed after the Jacobite Rising of 1715-6 as Rob had been accused of treason.

Balgonie Castle

NO 313007   LR: 59
Off A911, 3.5 miles E of Glenrothes, Balgonie, Fife.

Balgonie Castle consists of a fine 14th-century keep, with a crenellated battlement and corbiestepped gables, with in a courtyard enclosing ranges of buildings, many of which have been restored. The castle was garrisoned and no doubt looted by Rob Roy MacGregor and 200 clansmen in 1716 during the Jacobite Rising.

***Open all year, daily 10.00-17.00, unless hired for a
private function, including Christmas & New Year.***
Guided tours. Picnic area. Disabled access to ground
floor. Car and coach parking. Weddings. £.
Tel: 01592 750119   Fax: 01592 753103

Balquhidder Kirkyard

NN 535209   LR: 57

*Off A84, 14 miles NW of Callander, Balquhidder
Kirkyard, Balquhidder, Stirlingshire.*

Rob was captured here in 1717 by the Duke of Montrose
although he later escaped. At the west end of the burial
ground are three burial slabs, enclosed by railings, for Rob
Roy MacGregor (who died on 28 December 1734), his
wife, and two of his sons. His stone has a sword roughly
carved on it.

The old parish church is ruined, while on the north wall
of the modern church is St Angus's Stone, which dates
from the 8th century. The church has a 17th-century bell
from the old church, and old Gaelic bibles.

Access at all reasonable times.
Parking nearby.

Balquhidder Kirkyard.

Bannachra Castle

NS 343843   LR: 56

Off B831 or B832, 3 miles E of Helensburgh, Bannachra, Dunbartonshire.

Bannachra Castle is a ruined tower house of the Colquhouns. Sir Humphrey Colquhoun was besieged here by a party of MacGregors and MacFarlanes in 1592. He was shot with an arrow through a window, on his way to bed, having been illuminated and betrayed by a treacherous servant. This and other events led to bad blood between the MacGregors and Colquhouns, which came to battle at Glen Fruin in 1603. The Colquhouns were defeated and slaughtered, but the MacGregors were proscribed by James VI, and their chief executed a year later.

Blair Castle

NN 867662   LR: 43

Off A9, 5.5 miles NW of Pitlochry, 1 mile NW of Blair Atholl, Perthshire.

White-washed and castellated, Blair Castle is a rambling mansion of the Dukes of Atholl, and incorporates the 13th-century Comyn's Tower.

In 1653 the castle was besieged, captured and partly destroyed with gunpowder by Cromwell. The castle was sufficiently complete, however, to be garrisoned by 'Bonnie Dundee', John Graham of Claverhouse, in 1689, and it was here that his body was brought after the Battle of Killiecrankie. The family were made Marquises, then Dukes of Atholl in 1703. The Duke of Atholl has the distinction of having the only remaining private army in Europe.

Bonnie Prince Charlie stayed here in 1745, and Blair is the last castle in Britain to have been besieged.

Open 10.00-18.00 daily Apr-Oct; last admission 17.00.
32 interesting rooms. Collections of paintings, tapestries, arms, armour, china, costumes and Jacobite mementoes. Fine Georgian plasterwork. Guided tours at busy times. Gift shop. Licensed restaurant. Tearoom. Walled garden. Picnic area. Deer park. Disabled access & facilities. Car and coach parking. Group concessions. ££.
Tel: 01796 481207   Fax: 01796 481487
Email: blair@great-houses-scotland.co.uk
Web: www.great-houses-scotland.co.uk/blair

Breadalbane Folklore Centre

NN 573324   LR: 51

On A827, Falls of Dochart, Killin, Stirlingshire.

The centre features the history of local clans including the MacGregors. There is also a tourist information centre, and features include a water wheel, healing stones, and displays on Killin, Breadalbane and St Fillan.

Open Mar-May, daily 10.00-17.00; Jun daily 10.00-18.00; Jul-Aug daily 9.30-18.30; Sep, daily 10.00-18.00; Oct, daily 10.00-17.00; closed Nov-Jan; Feb open wknds only, 10.00-16.00.
Guided tours by request. Explanatory displays. Gift shop. WC. Disabled access. Induction loop. Car and coach parking. Group concessions. £.
Tel: 01567 820254   Fax: 01567 820764

Buchanan Castle

NS 463886   LR: 57

Off B807, 0.5 miles W of Drymen, Stirlingshire.

Buchanan Castle is a huge castellated ruin which incorporates an ancient castle.

 It was the seat of the Buchanans, but in 1682 was sold to the Graham Marquises of Montrose. They were made Dukes in 1707, and the 1st Duke spent much of his time trying to track down Rob Roy MacGregor. It was burnt down in 1850, and a new house built in 1854, designed by William Burn. The gardens were modelled by Capability Brown, but have been swallowed up by a golf course.

Corryarklet

NN 375095   LR: 56

Off B829, 15 miles NW of Aberfoyle, Corryarklet, Loch Arklet, Stirlingshire.

Rob Roy was married to Helen Mary MacGregor of Comer here in 1693. Rob had property at Inversnaid, which is some miles to the west near the east bank of Loch Lomond.

Craigrostan

NN 337044   LR: 56

Off B829 or B837, 11.5 miles NW of Aberfoyle, 4 miles N of Rowardennan, E side of Loch Lomond, Craig Roystan.

Rob Roy had a house here, but it was burnt in March 1713 by forces, under Graham of Killearn, acting for the Duke of Montrose. Montrose claimed Rob's property as Rob had been declared bankrupt and had been outlawed after £1000 of Montrose's money had been stolen by one of Rob's men. Rob Roy was not here, but his wife and children were turned out of their home, and Mary may have been raped and branded. She fled to Portnellan on Loch Katrine.

Creag an Taxman, Balquhidder

NN 516213   LR: 51

Off A84, 5 miles W of Lochearnhead, 1 mile W of Balquhidder, N of Tulloch, Stirlingshire.

A cave here is said to have been one of Rob Roy's hiding places.

Culloden Moor

NTS   NH 745450   LR: 27

On B9006, 5 miles E of Inverness, Culloden, Highland.

It was here on the bleak moor of Drumossie that on 16 April 1746 the Jacobite army of Bonnie Prince Charlie was crushed by Hanoverian forces led by the Duke of Cum-berland – the last major bat-tle to be fought on British soil. The Jacobites were tired and hungry, and the Hanoverians had a better equipped and larger army: the battle turned into a rout and many Jacobites were slaughtered after the battle. James Mor and the Mac-Gregors fought here but survived. Sites of interest include Old Leanach Cottage, Graves of the Clans, Wells of the Dead, Memorial Cairn, and Field of the English.

Site open daily all year; visitor centre and shop open Feb -Mar & Nov-30 Dec except 24/26 Dec 10.00-16.00; Apr-Oct daily 9.00-18.00; last admission to exhibition area 30 mins before closing; audiovisual show closes 30 mins before Visitor Centre.

Guided tours available in summer. Visitor centre with audiovisual programme. Gift shop. Restaurant. WC. Disabled access to visitor centre, WC and facilities. Car and coach parking. Group concessions. £.

Tel: 01463 790607   Fax: 01463 794294
Web: www.nts.org.uk

Drummond Castle

NN 844181   LR: 58

Off A822, 2.5 miles SW of Crieff, Drummond, Perthshire.

Built on a rocky outcrop, Drummond Castle consists of a large mansion and castle. It was owned by the Drummond Earls of Perth. The castle was badly damaged by Cromwell in the 1650s, and slighted after having been occupied by Hanoverian troops during the Jacobite Rising of 1715. The 5th Earl had commanded the Jacobite cavalry at the Battle of Sheriffmuir that year, and the 6th commanded the left wing of the Jacobite army at the Battle of Culloden in 1746. The family was forfeited as a result, although the Earldom of Perth was recovered by them in 1853, as was Stobhall where they now live.

Rob Roy MacGregor converted to catholicism, and his confession was heard here in 1730.

The castle passed to the Willoughbys, then the Earl of Ancaster. The castle and magnificent formal garden featured in the film version of 'Rob Roy'. The terraces overlook a magnificent parterre, celebrating the saltire and family heraldry, surrounding a famous sundial by John Milne, Master Mason to Charles I.

Castle not open. Gardens open Easter & May-Oct 14.00-18.00; last admission 17.00.
Gift shop. Disabled partial access. WC. Car and coach parking.
Tel: 01764 681257/433   Fax: 01764 681550

Dunkeld

HS   NO 025426   LR: 52
Off A923, Dunkeld, Perthshire.

Standing in the picturesque village of Dunkeld on the banks
of the Tay, the 14th-century choir of the cathedral is still
used as the parish church, although the nave is now ruinous.

 Dunkeld was besieged by the Jacobites in 1689 after the
Battle of Killiecrankie. The Cameronian garrison managed
to hold the town, within the cathedral precinct, although
most of the town was burnt, and had to be subsequently
rebuilt. The Jacobites and the Cameronians lost many men,
but it was the Jacobites who withdrew.

**Cathedral: ruined nave and tower open all year; choir
used as parish church: open Apr-Sep, Mon-Sat 9.00-
18.30, Sun 14.0-18.30.**
Sales area. Picnic area. WC. Disabled access. Parking
nearby.
Tel: 01350 723205

Edinburgh Castle

HS   NT 252735   LR: 66
Off A1, in the centre of Edinburgh.

Standing on a high rock, Edinburgh Castle was one of the
strongest and most important fortresses in Scotland. The
oldest building is a small Norman chapel of the early 12th
century, dedicated to St Margaret, wife of Malcolm Canmore. The fine Norman chancel arch survives, and a copy
of St Margaret's gospel book can be seen here.

 In 1566 Mary, Queen of Scots, gave birth to the future

James VI in the castle. After her abdication, it was held on her behalf, until English help forced it to surrender in 1573. The castle was captured in 1640 after a three-month siege by the Covenanters, and Cromwell besieged it throughout the autumn of 1650. The Jacobites failed to take it in both the 1715 and 1745 Risings, and many of the present buildings date from the 17th and 18th centuries.

Donald Glas, Rob Roy's father was imprisoned here for several years after the Jacobite Rising of 1689, as was the chief of the MacGregors after the 1745 Rebellion. James Mor and Robin Oig were also imprisoned here in 1752 for their part in the abduction and forced marriage of Jean Kay. James Mor managed to escape with help from his daughter, but Robin Oig was executed.

The castle is the home of the Scottish crown jewels, and the Stone of Destiny – on which the Kings of Scots were inaugurated – and is an interesting complex of buildings with spectacular views over the capital.

Open daily all year: Apr-Sep 9.30-17.15; Oct-Mar 9.30-16.15, castle closes 45 mins after last ticket is sold; times

may be altered during Tattoo and state occasions; closed Christmas & New Year.
Explanatory displays. Guided tours. Gift shop. Restaurant. WC. Disabled access. Visitors with a disability can be taken to the top of the castle by a courtesy vehicle; ramps and lift access to Crown Jewels and Stone of Destiny. Car and coach parking (except during Tattoo). £££.
Tel: 0131 225 9846

Eilean Donan Castle

NG 881259   LR: 33
On A87, 8 miles E of Kyle of Lochalsh, Dornie, Highland.

One of the most beautifully situated of all Scottish castles, Eilean Donan Castle is a fine castellated building, although it was completely rebuilt in the 20th century.

It was a property of the Mackenzies, but held for them by the MacRaes. William Mackenzie, 5th Earl of Seaforth, had it garrisoned with Spanish troops during the Jacobite

rising of 1719, but three frigates battered it into submission with cannon, and it was blown up from within when more than 300 barrels of gunpowder were detonated. The ghost of one of the Spanish troops, killed either at the castle or the nearby battle of Glenshiel, is said to haunt the castle.

The Battle of Glenshiel took place at the head of Loch Duich, near Shiel Bridge, and the site is marked by an information board. The castle has mementoes of Bonnie Prince Charlie and James VIII and III.

Open Apr-Oct, daily 10.00-17.30.
Guided tours available. Visitor centre. New exhibitions. Gift shop. Tearoom. WC and disabled WC. Car and coach parking. Group concessions. *££.*
Tel: 01599 555202   Fax: 01599 555262

Eilean Molach, Loch Katrine

NN 488083   LR: 57

Off A821, 5 miles N of Aberfoyle, Eilean Molach, Loch Katrine, Stirlingshire.

The island in the loch was used as a stronghold by the MacGregors in the middle of the 16th century. It does not appear to have had walls as the steepness of the banks made it an ideal refuge. There was a lodge here in the 19th century, which was destroyed by fire.

Falkland Palace

NTS   NO 254075   LR: 59

Off A912, 4 miles N of Glenrothes, Falkland, Fife.

Falkland Palace is a fortified but comfortable royal residence, which was remodelled in Renaissance style. It consists of ranges of buildings around an open courtyard. The Chapel Royal, with fine mullioned windows, has a 16th-century oak screen at one end, and the painted ceiling dates from 1633. The restored cross house contains a refurbished room, reputedly the King's Room, where James V died in 1542. Rob Roy

MacGregor was based here in 1716 during the Jacobite Rising.

Open Apr (or Good Friday if earlier)-Oct 11.00-17.30, Sun 13.30-17.30; last admission to Palace 16.30, garden 17.00; groups at other times by appt.

Explanatory displays. Gift shop. Visitor centre. Picnic area. Extensive gardens. Real tennis court. WC. Disabled access. Tape tour for visually impaired. Car parking nearby. ££.

Tel: 01337 857397   Fax: 01337 857980

Finlarig Castle

NN 575338   LR: 51

Off A827, 0.5 miles NE of Killin, W end of Loch Tay, Finlarig, Stirlingshire.

Finlarig Castle, a 17th-century Z-plan tower house, is now

ruined. The castle was built in 1621-9 by the Campbell 'Black Duncan of the Cowl' or 'Black Duncan of the Castles'. It was held by the Campbell Earls of Breadalbane, and Rob Roy MacGregor was sheltered here in 1713. Close by is said to be a beheading pit, containing a block and a sunken cavity for the head. Noble folk were executed in the pit, while the common people were hanged on a neighbouring oak tree.

Glencoe

NTS NN 127564 LR: 41

On A82, 17 miles S of Fort William, Glencoe, Highlands.

Glencoe, one of the most picturesque and accessible parts of Scotland, was the site of the infamous massacre in 1692, executed by government forces under Robert Campbell of Glenlyon, Rob Roy's uncle. Thirty eight members of the MacDonalds of Glencoe, including their chief MacIain, were slaughtered by men from the garrison at Fort William, who had been billeted on the MacDonalds. One of the sites of the massacre at Inverglen can be visited; as can the Signal Rock, where the signal was reputedly given to

begin the massacre. A visitor centre includes a video programme on the massacre. It also features an exhibition on
the history of mountaineering.

*Site open all year; visitor centre, shop and snack bar open
Apr (or Good Friday if earlier)-Oct, 10.00-17.00; open
19 May-Aug, daily 9.30-17.30; last admission 30 mins
before closing.*

Video programme on the massacre. Exhibition on the
history of mountaineering. Guided walks in glen. Gift
shop. Snack bar. WC. Picnic area. Disabled access to
visitor centre. Walks. Climbing. Car and coach parking.
Group concessions. £ (visitor centre).

Tel: 01855 811307   Fax: 01855 811772

Glen Fruin

NS 276894   LR: 56

*Off A814, 3 miles SE of Garelochhead, Auchengaich, Glen
Fruin, Dunbartonshire.*

The site of the battle near Auchengaich, fought between

the MacGregors and the Colquhouns of Luss on 7 February 1603. Although the MacGregors were outnumbered, they turned the tables on the Colquhouns, and some 140 or more of the latter clan were slain in the following rout. The battle resulted in dire retribution for the MacGregors. The clan, and even their name, were proscribed by James VI in April and by March the following year 35 of the clan had been executed, including Alasdair, the chief.

Glengyle Castle

NN 385135   LR: 56

Off B829, 13 miles NW of Glengyle, N end of Loch Katrine, 2.5 miles NW of Stronachlachar, at Glengyle, Stirlingshire.

There was apparently a castle here, some remains of which survived in the 19th century. It was a property of the MacGregors of Glengyle, who were chiefs of the MacGregors. Rob Roy's father, Donald Glas, was styled 'of Glengyle'.

Glenshiel

NTS   NH 962211   LR: 33

Off A87, 16 miles E of Kyle of Lochalsh, Morvich, Kintail, Highland.

The picturesque estate of Kintail and Morvich covers 17422 acres and includes the Five Sisters of Kintail, four of which are Munros (over 3000 feet), as well as the Falls of Glomach. This is where the Battle of Glenshiel took place in 1719. The Jacobite army, which included about 300 Spaniards, was defeated by government forces. About 5 miles east of the village near the main road is an information board. Access to the mountains is best gained from the countryside centre at Morvich.

Access at all reasonable times. Countryside centre at Morvich open May-Sep, daily 9.00-22.00.
Explanatory board. Sales area. WC. Parking. Outdoor centre: accommodation. Caravan site. £.
Tel: 01599 511231   Fax: 01599 511417

Glen Shira

NN 151170   LR: 56

Off A83, 6 miles NE of Inveraray, at the head of Glen Shira, Argyll.

The ruined building is believed to be where Rob Roy stayed after being outlawed. He was offered the property by the Campbell Duke of Argyll.

Glenstrae Castle

NN 138296   LR: 50

Off B8077, 2.5 miles north-west of Dalmally, north of Castles Farm, Glenstrae, Argyll.

Site of castle, a property of the MacGregors of Glenstrae from the beginning of the 15th century until 1604. The property then passed to the Campbells with the proscription of the MacGregors after they had defeated the Colquhouns and their allies at the Battle of Glen Fruin the previous year. The castle was apparently burnt in 1611 by Sir Duncan Campbell.

Highland Folk Museum, Kingussie

NH 758007   LR: 35

On A86, 12 miles SW of Aviemore, Duke Street, Kingussie, Strathspey, Highland; also at Newtonmore (2.5 miles away).

Covering some 400 years of Highland life, the museum has a comprehensive collection of social history material, displayed in realistic settings and reconstructed buildings, such as a blackhouse from Lewis, a click mill and a smoke house. Displays include traditional farming, farm machinery and country crafts, as well as domestic life, costume and furniture. The museum gives some idea how Highlanders lived in the time of Rob Roy.

There are two sites: Kingussie and Newtonmore.

Open all year: Easter-Aug Mon-Sat 10.30-17.30, Sun 13.00-17.00; Sep/Oct Mon- Fri 10.30-16.30 Nov-Easter, Mon-Fri 10.00-15.00; closed Christmas and New Year. (Newtonmore site opening times vary slightly). Season ticket (as part of NMS scheme) also available.
Guided tours (hourly). Explanatory displays. Gift shop. Picnic area. WC. Disabled access. Car and coach parking.
Tel: 01540 661307   Fax: 01540 661631
Email: highland.folk@highland.gov.uk
Web: www.highlandfolk.com

Inveraray Castle

NN 096093   LR: 56

Off A83, N of Inveraray, Argyll.

Inveraray Castle, a large classical mansion with corner towers and turrets, was begun in 1744 for the Campbell Dukes of Argyll. The castle, which is still the seat of the Dukes of Argyll, houses many interesting rooms, with collections of

tapestries and paintings, and superb displays of weapons. Rob Roy MacGregor's sporran and dirk handle are on display. The Clan Room features information of special interest to members of Clan Campbell.

Open Apr-Oct, Mon- Thu & Sat 10.00-13.00 and 14.00-17.45, Sun 13.00-17.45, closed Fri; Jul and Aug, Mon-Sat 10.00-17.45, Sun 13.00-17.45; last admissions 12.30 and 17.00.

Guided tours. Collections of tapestries and paintings. Displays of weapons. Gift shop. Tea room. WC. Picnic area. Disabled access to ground floor only. Car and coach parking. Group concessions. ££.

Tel: 01499 302203   Fax: 01499 302421
Email: enquiries@inveraray-castle.com
Web: www.inveraray-castle.com

Inverlochlarig

NN 438191   LR: 56

Off A84, 6 miles W of Balquhidder, Inverlochlarig, Stirlingshire.

The site of one of the houses of Rob Roy MacGregor. Some remains may be built into a bothy.

Inversnaid

NN 348097   LR: 56

Off B829, 16 miles NW of Aberfoyle, west end of Glen Arklet, at Garrison, Stirlingshire.

Not much remains of a barracks, dating from 1718.
   Inversnaid was owned by Rob Roy MacGregor, and he may have been given the property by his father, Donald Glas of Glengyle. The property was seized by the Duke of Montrose after Rob had been declared an outlaw and Craigrostan burnt. The Duke had a barracks built on the site after the Jacobite Rising of 1715, reputedly on the site of Rob's house. Rob Roy's men attacked the workmen during construction, and the barracks were burnt in 1745. The barracks were commanded by General Wolfe, before he was a general, but were abandoned by 1800. In 1820 part of the building was used as an inn, but it had been demolished by 1828.

Kilbryde Castle

NN 756036   LR: 57

Off A820, 3 miles NW of Dunblane, Kilbryde, Stirlingshire.

Kilbryde Castle is a 16th-century L-plan tower house, and

was originally a property of the Graham Earls of Menteith. The property was sold to the Campbells of Aberuchill in 1669, one of whom, Sir Colin, Lord Aberuchill of Session, was prominent in his activities against Rob Roy MacGregor, but still had to pay blackmail to be left alone by the MacGregors. The castle was remodelled and extended around 1877.

The gardens, which have been restored and developed, are open to the public.

Garden open to the public all year; castle not open.
Parking.
Tel: 01786 824505   Fax: 01786 825405

Kilchurn Castle

HS   NN 133276   LR: 50
Off A85, 2 miles W of Dalmally, Kilchurn, Argyll.

A picturesque and much photographed ruin, Kilchurn Castle is a ruinous courtyard castle of the 15th century,

consisting of a rectangular keep, which was extended with ranges of buildings in the 16th century.

The lands originally belonged to the MacGregors, and stand near to Glenstrae. The MacGregors may have had a stronghold here, but this area was acquired by the Campbells of Glenorchy, who then held the castle. Kilchurn was strengthened and improved by Black Duncan of the Seven Castles, Sir Duncan Campbell, at the end of the 16th century. The Campbells withstood a two-day siege in 1654 by General Middleton before he retreated before Monck's Cromwellian forces. The castle was inhabited by the Campbells until 1740 when they moved to Taymouth. Kilchurn was garrisoned by Hanoverian troops in 1745, but was ruinous by 1770. The castle was put into the care of the state in 1953, and has been consolidated and repaired.

There are regular sailings from Loch Awe pier to Kilchurn by steamer – phone ferry company 01838 200400/ 200449.

Open Apr-Sep, daily 9.30-18.30.
Parking nearby.
Tel: 0131 668 8800   Fax: 0131 668 8888

Killiecrankie

NTS   NN 917627   LR: 43
On B8079, 3 miles N of Pitlochry, Perthshire.

Set in a fine and picturesque wooded gorge, it was here in 1689 that the Jacobites, led by John Graham of Claverhouse, Viscount Dundee, defeated a government army. Rob Roy and his father fought at the battle. Claverhouse was mortally wounded at the battle, and the Jacobites disbanded after failing to capture Dunkeld. There is the 'Soldier's Leap', where one government soldier escaped from Jacobite forces by jumping across the River Garry. Exhibition in the visitor centre features the battle, with models and maps, and there are also displays on natural history.

Site open all year; visitor centre, shop and snack bar open 1 Apr (or Good Friday if earlier)-Oct 10.00-17.30.
Exhibition. Gift shop. Tearoom. WC. Disabled WC. Car park. £.
Tel: 01796 473233

Loch Dochart Castle

NN 407257   LR: 51

Off A85, 11 miles W of Killin, Loch Dochart, Stirlingshire.

Standing on an island in the loch, Loch Dochart Castle is a ruined 16th-century tower house with other buildings. It was built by Sir Duncan Campbell of Glenorchy, Black Duncan of the Castles, between 1585 and 1631, but was burnt out in 1646. The ruins have been cleared and consolidated.

The castle is traditionally associated with Rob Roy MacGregor.

Logierait Castle

NN 977513   LR: 52

Off A825, 6 miles N of Dunkeld, Logierait, Perthshire.

Only a ditch and foundations remain of a 14th-century castle. Rob Roy MacGregor escaped from here in 1717 after being sized at Dunkeld House. He got his guards drunk and then fled on a servant's horse. In 1745 the Jacobites used the castle to confine 1600 prisoners captured after the Battle of Prestonpans.

There is a memorial to the Murray 6th Duke of Atholl on the site.

Megginch Castle

NO 242246   LR: 53

About 8 miles E of Perth, E of A85, Megginch, Perthshire.

Surrounded by woodlands, Megginch Castle is an altered L-plan tower house, later altered and extended.

  It was a property of the Hays, but was sold to the Drummonds of Lennoch in 1646. The 3rd Drummond of Megginch was the first member of Parliament for Perthshire in the Union parliament of 1707, but was unsuccessful in trying to hunt down Rob Roy MacGregor. The Drummond family still live at the house, and there are extensive gardens with 1000-year-old yews, 16th-century rose garden, kitchen garden, topiary and 16th-century physic garden.

  The courtyard of the castle was used for filming part of the film version of 'Rob Roy' with Liam Neeson in 1994. The gardens, but not the castle, are regularly open in the summer.

Castle not open; gardens open Jun- Sep, daily 14.30-17.00. Other times by prior arrangement
Guided tours by arrangement and extra charge. Disabled partial access. Car and coach parking. £.
Tel: 01821 642222   Fax: 01821 642708

Mercat Cross, Edinburgh

NT 257737   LR: 66

Off A1, Royal Mile, W of St Giles Cathedral, Edinburgh.

The chief of the MacGregors, Alasdair Roy, was executed here in 1604 after the clan had been proscribed following the slaughter of the Colquhouns at Glen Fruin.

Accessible at all times.

Portnellan

NN 406119   LR: 56

*Off A821, 14 miles W of Callander, on track, N side of
Loch Katrine, Portnellan, Stirlingshire.*

The small walled burial ground contains several grave slabs,
and was used by the MacGregors. The earliest stone is dated
1699. Mary MacGregor fled here after being evicted from
her house at Craigrostan. Graham of Killearn, Montrose's
factor, was seized and brought here by Rob Roy, and he
was then said to have been held on an island in the loch.

Prestonpans Battle Cairn

NT 403744   LR: 66

Off A198, E of Prestonpans, East Lothian.

The site of the Jacobite victory in 1745, led by Bonnie
Prince Charlie, over a government army under Sir John
Cope. The MacGregors fought at the battle, and were responsible for the killing of Colonel Gardiner. James Mor
was wounded, but went on to fight at the Battle of Culloden. A memorial cairn marks the site.

Access to site at all reasonable times.

Rob Roy and Trossachs Visitor Centre, Callander

NN 628079   LR: 57

*On A84, 16 miles NW of Stirling, Ancaster Square,
Callander, Stirlingshire.*

The centre relates the story of Scotland's most famous

outlaw, Rob Roy MacGregor, in a multimedia theatre. His life is explained in the carefully researched 'Life and Times' interactive exhibition, as well as a 20-minute film. There is a Highland cottage, and also detailed visitor information on the Trossachs, as well as a Scottish bookshop.

Open Mar-May and Oct-Dec, daily 10.00-17.00; Jun-Sep, daily 9.30-19.00. Last admission 45-60 mins before closing.

Explanatory displays. Gift shop. Play area. WC. Disabled access. Car parking. Group concessions. £.

Tel: 01877 330342   Fax: 01877 330784

Rob Roy's Cave, Inversnaid

NN 332100   LR: 56

Off B829, 13.5 miles NW of Aberfoyle, 1 mile N of Inversnaid, E side of Loch Lomond, Stirlingshire.

The cave is associated with Rob Roy, who is said to have planned his raids and forays from here. The cave is also believed to have been used by Robert the Bruce in the dark days after he was crowned king at Scone in 1306. He was a hunted fugitive at this time. On the West Highland Way, a path from Glasgow to Fort William.

   Further down Loch Lomond is Rob Roy's Prison [NN 328028].

Rob Roy's Cave, Loch Ard

NN 480012   LR: 57

Off B829, 3 miles W of Aberfoyle, Loch Ard, Stirlingshire.

The cave here is traditionally associated with Rob Roy MacGregor.

Rob Roy's Statue, Peterculter

NJ 836009   LR: 38

On A93, 6.5 miles W of Aberdeen, W end of Peterculter, Aberdeenshire.

The statue of Rob Roy stands above the Leuchar Burn, and can be seen from the bridge on the main road. The original statue was taken from the figure head of a whaling boat, but it has since been replaced.

Access at all reasonable times.
Parking nearby.

Rob Roy's Statue, Stirling

NS 795935   LR: 57

Off A872, below the town hall, centre of Stirling.

The statue is based on a contemporary illustrations, which is believed to be of Rob Roy MacGregor. The statue is by Benno Schotz.

Rob Roy's statue, Stirling.

Rossdhu Castle

NS 361896   LR: 56

Off A82, 2 miles S of Luss, near Rossdhu House, near shore of Loch Lomond, Dunbartonshire.

Rossdhu Castle is a ruined 16th-century tower house of the Colquhouns of Luss. James Colquhoun led his clan to defeat in a battle with the MacGregors in Glen Fruin in 1603. The tower was mostly demolished to provide materials for the nearby Rossdhu House, which was completed in 1774.

Scone Palace

NO 114267   LR: 58

Off A93, N of Perth, Scone, Perthshire.

Scone Palace, a large castellated mansion dating from 1802 and designed by William Atkinson, incorporates part of the palace built by the Ruthvens in the 1580s, itself probably created out of the Abbot's Lodging. Scone passed to the Murrays in 1600, and the family were made Viscounts Stormont in 1602, and Earls of Mansfield in 1776. James

VIII and III held 'court' here in 1716, and Bonnie Prince Charlie visited in 1745.

Open Easter-4th Mon Oct daily 9.30-17.15; last admission 16.45; other times by appt.
Fine collections of furniture, clocks, needlework and porcelain. Gift shops. Restaurant. Tearoom. WC. Picnic area. 100 acres of wild gardens. Maze. Adventure playground. Meetings and conferences. Disabled access to state rooms & restaurant. Car and coach parking. Group concessions. £££.
Tel: 01738 552300 Fax: 01738 552588
Email: SCONEPALACE@CQM.CO.UK
Web: www.sconepalace.co.uk

Sheriffmuir

NN 830028 LR: 57
Off A9, 3 miles E of Dunblane, Sheriffmuir, Stirlingshire.

The site of the battle fought on 13 November 1715 between Jacobites under the Earl of Mar and a Hanoverian army led by the Duke of Argyll. The left wings of each army were defeated by the right wing of the other, while the centres did not fight. The Jacobites were left holding the field, but the battle was a turning point and support dwindled so that by early 1716 the rising was over.

   Rob Roy and his men arrived at the battle as it was ending, and took no part in the fighting. Some believe that he refused to fight, but his men had already marched many miles that day. It also seems unlikely that, although he was a fine leader, Rob could have changed the outcome at Sheriffmuir.

   The Gathering Stone [NN 810021] is traditionally where the Jacobite army was marshalled, and the White Stone [NN 806042] is also known as MacGregor's Stone and is traditionally associated with the battle.

Stirling Castle

HS   NS 790940   LR: 57

Off A872, Upper Castle Hill, in Stirling.

One of the most important and powerful castles in Scotland, Stirling Castle stands on a high rock, and consists of a courtyard castle, which dates in part from the 12th century.

Features of interest are the Great Hall, Chapel Royal, the King's Old Buildings, kitchens, the wall walk and the nearby 'King's Knot', the earthworks of a magnificent ornamental garden

The castle is an a strategically important position, and was much involved in the warfare of the times. It was also a royal residence, and Mary, Queen of Scots, was crowned in the old chapel in 1543, and the future James VI was baptised here in 1566. James VI stayed here in 1617, as did Charles I in 1633, and Charles II in 1650. In 1651 the castle was besieged by Monck for Cromwell, but it surrendered after a few days because of a mutiny in the garrison.

Donald Glas, Rob Roy's father was imprisoned here for three months before being taken to Edinburgh. The castle was in a poor state of repair in the 18th century, but the garrison harried the Jacobites during both the 1715 and 1745 Risings, and the Jacobites besieged the castle after the Battle of Falkirk in 1746, although not very successfully.

There is an exhibition of life in the royal palace, introductory display, and the medieval kitchen display. Museum of Argyll and Sutherland Highlanders tells the story of the regiment from 1794 to the present day, and includes uni-

forms, silver, paintings, colours, pipe banners and com-
mentaries.

***Open all year: Apr-Sep daily 9.30-17.15; Oct-Mar daily
9.30-16.15; castle closes 45 mins after last ticket sold –
joint ticket with Argyll's Lodging.***
Guided tours are available and can be booked in
advance. Exhibition of life in the royal palace,
introductory display, medieval kitchen display. Museum
of Argyll & Sutherland Highlanders. Gift shop.
Restaurant. WC. Disabled access and WC. Car and coach
parking. Group concessions. *££*.
Tel: 01786 450000   Fax: 01786 464678

Stronmilchan

NN 153278   LR: 50

Off B8077, 1 mile NW of Dalmally, Stronmilchan, Argyll.

Site of castle, which has a moat and drawbridge. It was a
property of the MacGregors of Glenstrae. The last remains
were apparently demolished early in the 19th century.
  This may also have been known as Tigh Mor, or this may
refer to another building close by [NN 154288].

Index

Index